ISBN 0-8373-3840-9

C-3840   CAREER EXAMINATION SERIES

This is your
PASSBOOK® for...

Data Processing Assistant

Test Preparation Study Guide

Questions & Answers

NLC

NATIONAL LEARNING CORPORATION

PASSBOOK®

NOTICE

PASSBOOK SERIES®

THE *PASSBOOK SERIES*® has been created to prepare applicants and candidates for the ultimate academic battlefield—the examination room.

At some time in our lives, each and every one of us may be required to take an examination—for validation, matriculation, admission, qualification, registration, certification, or licensure.

Based on the assumption that every applicant or candidate has met the basic formal educational standards, has taken the required number of courses, and read the necessary texts, the *PASSBOOK SERIES*® furnishes the one special preparation which may assure passing with confidence, instead of failing with insecurity. Examination questions—together with answers—are furnished as the basic vehicle for study so that the mysteries of the examination and its compounding difficulties may be eliminated or diminished by a sure method.

This book is meant to help you pass your examination provided that you qualify and are serious in your objective.

The entire field is reviewed through the huge store of content information which is succinctly presented through a provocative and challenging approach—the question-and-answer method.

A climate of success is established by furnishing the correct answers at the end of each test.

You soon learn to recognize types of questions, forms of questions, and patterns of questioning. You may even begin to anticipate expected outcomes.

You perceive that many questions are repeated or adapted so that you gain acute insights, which may enable you to score many sure points.

You learn how to confront new questions, or types of questions, and to attack them confidently and work out the correct answers.

You note objectives and emphases, and recognize pitfalls and dangers, so that you may make positive educational adjustments.

Moreover, you are kept fully informed in relation to new concepts, methods, practices, and directions in the field.

You discover that you are actually taking the examination all the time: you are preparing for the examination by "taking" an examination, not by reading extraneous and/or supererogatory textbooks.

In short, this PASSBOOK®, used directedly, should be an important factor in helping you to pass your test.

DATA PROCESSING ASSISTANT

DUTIES

Assists in handling data processing, including the operation of microcomputers with video terminals, floppy disk drives, and tractor or page feed printers in accordance with programmed instructions. Records, edits, stores, and revises reports, statistical and accounting data, and other textual materials, and supervises the transcribing of data from source documents to magnetic tape or directly into a computer. The work is performed under general supervision of a higher level employee in the organization with leeway allowed for exercise of independent judgment in carrying out details of the work. Supervision is exercised over the work of data entry machine operators. Does related work as required.

SUBJECT OF EXAMINATION

The written test will be designed to test for knowledge, skills, and/or abilities in such areas as:
1. Fundamentals of microcomputer systems;
2. Use and operation of microcomputers and related peripheral equipment;
3. Reading and interpreting instructions relating to file coding and the execution of microcomputer software; and
4. Preparing written material.

HOW TO TAKE A TEST

I. YOU MUST PASS AN EXAMINATION
  A. *WHAT EVERY CANDIDATE SHOULD KNOW*
      Examination applicants often ask us for help in preparing for
the written test. What can I study in advance?
What kinds of questions will be asked? How will the test be given?
How will the papers be graded?
      As an applicant for a civil service examination, you may be won-
dering about some of these things. Our purpose here is to suggest effective methods of advance study and to describe civil service examinations.
      Your chances for success on this examination can be increased if
you know how to prepare. Those "pre-examination jitters" can be reduced if you know what to expect. You can even experience an adven-
ture in good citizenship if you know why civil service examinations
are given.
  B. *WHY ARE CIVIL SERVICE EXAMINATIONS GIVEN?*
      Civil service examinations are important to you in two ways. As
a citizen, you want public jobs filled by employees who know how to
do their work. As a job-seeker, you want a fair chance to compete for
that job on an equal footing with other candidates. The best known
means of accomplishing this two-fold goal is the competitive examination.
      Examinations are widely publicized throughout the nation. They
may be administered for jobs in federal, state, city, municipal, town,
or village governments or agencies.
      Any citizen may apply, with some limitations, such as the age or
residence of applicants. Your experience and education may be reviewed
to see whether you meet the requirements for the particular examination. When these requirements exist, they are reasonable and are applied consistently to all applicants. Thus, a competitive examination
may cause you some uneasiness now, but it is your privilege and safe-
guard.
  C. *HOW ARE CIVIL SERVICE EXAMINATIONS DEVELOPED?*
      Examinations are carefully written by trained technicians who
are specialists in the field known as "psychological measurement,"
in consultation with recognized authorities in the field of work that
the test will cover. These experts recommend the subject matter areas
or skills to be tested; only those knowledges or skills important to
your success on the job are included. The most reliable books and
source materials available are used as references. Together, the experts and technicians judge the difficulty level of the questions.
      Test technicians know how to phrase questions so that the prob-
lem is clearly stated. Their ethics do not permit "trick" or "catch"
questions. Questions may have been tried out on sample groups, or
subjected to statistical analysis, to determine their usefulness.
      Written tests are often used in combination with performance
tests, ratings of training and experience, and oral interviews. All
of these measures combine to form the best known means of finding
the right man for the right job.

II. HOW TO PASS THE WRITTEN TEST

A. NATURE OF THE EXAMINATION

To prepare intelligently for civil service examinations, you should know how they differ from school examinations you have taken. In school you were assigned certain definite pages to read or subjects to cover. The examination questions were quite detailed and usually emphasized memory. Civil service examinations, on the other hand, try to discover your present ability to perform the duties of a position, plus your potentiality to learn these duties. In other words, a civil service examination attempts to predict how successful you will be. Questions cover such a broad area that they cannot be as minute and detailed as school examination questions.

In the public service similar kinds of work, or positions, are grouped together in one "class." This process is known as "position-classification." All the positions in a class are paid according to the salary range for that class. One class title covers all these positions, and they are all tested by the same examination.

B. FOUR BASIC STEPS

1. Study the Announcement.--How, then, can you know what subjects to study? Our best answer is: "Learn as much as possible about the class of positions for which you have applied." The examination will test the knowledge, skills, and abilities needed to do the work.

Your most valuable source of information about the position you want is the official announcement of the examination. This announcement lists the training and experience qualifications. Check these standards and apply only if you come reasonably close to meeting them.

The brief description of the position in the examination announcement offers some clues to the subjects which will be tested. Think about the job itself. Review the duties in your mind. Can you perform them, or are there some in which you are rusty? Fill in the blank spots in your preparation.

Many jurisdictions preview the written test in the examination announcement by including a section called "Knowledge and Abilities Required," "Scope of Examination," or some similar heading. Here you will find out specifically what fields will be tested.

2. Review Your Own Background.-- Once you learn in general what the position is all about, and what you need to know to do the work, ask yourself which subjects you already know fairly well and which need improvement. You may wonder whether to concentrate on improving your strong areas or on building some background in your fields of weakness. When the announcement has specified "some knowledge" or "considerable knowledge," or has used adjectives such as "beginning principles of ...." or "advanced .....methods," you can get a clue as to the number and difficulty of questions to be asked in any given field. More questions, and hence broader coverage, would be included for those subjects which are more important in the work. Now weigh your strengths and weaknesses against the job requirements and prepare accordingly.

3. Determine the Level of the Position.-- Another way to tell how intensively you should prepare is to understand the level of the job for which you are applying. Is it the entering level? In other words, is this the position in which beginners in a field of work are hired? Or is it an intermediate or advanced level? Sometimes this is indicated by such words as "Junior" or "Senior" in the class title.Other jurisdictions use Roman numerals to designate the level: Clerk I,

Clerk II, for example. The word "Supervisor" sometimes appears in the title. If the level is not indicated by the title, check the description of duties. Will you be working under very close supervision, or will you have responsibility for independent decisions in this work?

4. Choose Appropriate Study Materials. -- Now that you know the subjects to be examined and the relative amount of each subject to be covered, you can choose suitable study materials. For beginning level jobs, or even advanced ones, if you have a pronounced weakness in some aspect of your training, read a modern, standard textbook in that field. Be sure it is up-to-date and has general coverage. Such books are normally available at your library, and the librarian will be glad to help you locate one. For entry level positions, questions of appropriate difficulty are chosen -- neither highly advanced questions, nor those too simple. Such questions require careful thought but not advanced training.

If the position for which you are applying is technical or advanced, you will read more advanced, specialized material. If you are already familiar with the basic principles of your field, elementary textbooks would waste your time. Concentrate on advanced textbooks and technical periodicals. Think through the concepts and review difficult problems in your field.

These are all general sources. You can get more ideas on your own initiative, following these leads. For example, training manuals and publications of the government agency which employs workers in your field can be useful, particularly for technical and professional positions. A letter or visit to the government department involved may result in more specific study suggestions, and certainly will provide you with a more definite idea of the exact nature of the position you are seeking.

III. KINDS OF TESTS

Tests are used for purposes other than measuring knowledge and ability to perform specified duties. For some positions, it is equally important to test ability to make adjustments to new situations or to profit from training. In others, basic mental abilities not dependent upon information are essential. Questions which test these things may not appear as pertinent to the duties of the position as those which test for knowledge and information. Yet they are often highly important parts of a fair examination. For very general questions, it is almost impossible to help you direct your study efforts. What we can do is to point out some of the more common of these general abilities needed in public service positions and describe some typical questions.

1. General Information

Broad, general information has been found useful for predicting job success in some kinds of work. This is tested in a variety of ways, from vocabulary lists to questions about current events. Basic background in some field of work, such as sociology or economics, may be sampled in a group of questions. Often these are principles which have become familiar to most persons through "exposure" rather than through formal training. It is difficult to advise you how to study for these questions; being alert to the world around you is our best suggestion.

2. Verbal Ability

An example of an ability needed in many positions is verbal or language ability. Verbal ability is, in brief, the ability to use and understand words. Vocabulary and grammar tests are typical measures of this ability. "Reading comprehension" or "paragraph interpretation" questions are common in many kinds of civil service tests. You are given a paragraph of written material and asked to find its central meaning.

3. Numerical Ability

Number skills can be tested by the familiar arithmetic problem, by checking paired lists of numbers to see which are alike and which are different, or by interpreting charts and graphs. In the latter test, a graph may be printed in the test booklet which you are asked to use as the basis for answering questions.

4. Observation

A popular test for law-enforcement positions is the observation test. A picture is shown to you for several minutes, then taken away. Questions about the picture test your ability to observe both details and larger elements.

5. Following Directions

In many positions in the public service, the employee must be able to carry out written instructions dependably and accurately. You may be given a chart with several columns, each column listing a variety of information. The questions require you to carry out directions involving the information given in the chart.

6. Skills and Aptitudes

Performance tests effectively measure some manual skills and aptitudes. When the skill is one in which you are trained, such as typing or shorthand, you can practice. These tests are often very much like those given in business school or high school courses. For many of the other skills and aptitudes, however, no short-time preparation can be made. Skills and abilities natural to you or that you have developed throughout your lifetime are being tested.

Many of the general questions just described provide all the data needed to answer the questions and ask you to use your reasoning ability to find the answers. Your best preparation for these tests, as well as for tests of facts and ideas, is to be at your physical and mental best. You, no doubt, have your own methods of getting into an exam-taking mood and keeping "in shape." The next section lists some ideas on this subject.

IV. KINDS OF QUESTIONS

Only rarely is the "essay" question, which you answer in narrative form, used in civil service tests. Civil service tests are usually of the short-answer type. Full instructions for answering these questions will be given to you at the examination. But in case this is your first experience with short-answer questions and separate answer sheets, here is what you need to know.

1. Multiple-Choice Questions

Most popular of the short-answer questions is the "multiple-choice" or "best-answer" question. It can be used, for example, to test for factual knowledge, ability to solve problems, or judgment in meeting situations found at work.

A multiple-choice question is normally one of three types:

(1) It can begin with an incomplete statement followed by several possible endings. You are to find the one ending which *best* completes the statement, although some of the others may not be entirely wrong.

(2) It can also be a complete statement in the form of a question which is answered by choosing one of the statements listed.

(3) It can be in the form of a problem -- again you select the best answer.

Here is an example of a multiple-choice question with a discussion which should give you some clues as to the method for choosing the right answer.

SAMPLE QUESTION:

When an employee has a complaint about his assignment, the action which will *best* help him overcome his difficulty is

    (A) to discuss his difficulty with his co-workers
    (B) to take the problem to the head of the organization
    (C) to take the problem to the person who gave him the assignment
    (D) to say nothing to anyone about his complaint

In answering this question you should study each of the choices to find which is best. Consider choice (A). Certainly an employee may discuss his complaint with fellow employees, but no change or improvement can result, and the complaint remains unsolved. Choice (B) is a poor choice since the head of the organization probably does not know what assignment you have been given, and taking your problem to him is known as "going over the head" of the supervisor. The supervisor, or person who made the assignment, is the person who can clarify it or correct any injustice. Choice (C) is, therefore, correct. To say nothing, as in choice (D), is unwise. Supervisors have an interest in knowing the problems employees are facing, and the employee is seeking a solution to his problem.

2. True-False Questions

The "true-false" or "right-wrong" form of question is sometimes used. Here a complete statement is given. Your problem is to decide whether the statement is right or wrong.

SAMPLE QUESTION:

A person-to-person long distance telephone call costs less than a station-to-station call to the same city.

This question is wrong, or "false," since person-to-person calls are more expensive.

This is not a complete list of all possible question forms, although most of the others are variations of these common types. You will always get complete directions for answering questions. Be sure you understand *how* to mark your answers -- ask questions until you do.

V. RECORDING YOUR ANSWERS

For an examination with very few applicants, you may be told to record your answers in the test booklet itself. Separate answer sheets are much more common. If this separate answer sheet is to be scored by machine -- and this is often the case -- it is highly important that you mark your answers correctly in order to get credit.

An electric test-scoring machine is often used in civil service offices because of the speed with which papers can be scored. Machine-scored answer sheets must be marked with a special pencil, which will be given to you. This pencil has a high graphite content which responds to the electrical scoring machine. As a matter of fact, stray dots may register as answers, so do not let your pencil rest on the answer sheet while you are pondering the correct answer. Also, if your pencil lead breaks or is otherwise defective, ask for another.

Since the answer sheet will be dropped in a slot in the scoring machine, be careful not to bend the corners or get the paper crumpled.

The answer sheet normally has five vertical columns of numbers, with 30 numbers to a column. These numbers correspond to the question numbers in your test booklet. After each number, going across the page, are four or five pairs of dotted lines. These short dotted lines have small letters or numbers above them. The first two pairs may also have a "T" and "F" above the letters. This indicates that the first two pairs only are to be used if the questions are of the true-false type. If the questions are multiple-choice, disregard this "T" and "F" completely, and pay attention only to the small number or letters.

Answer your questions in the manner of the sample that follows. Proceed in the sequential steps outlined below.

Assume that you are answering question 32, which is:

32. The largest city in the United States is:
 A. Washington, D.C.   B. New York City   C. Chicago
 D. Detroit   E. San Francisco

1. Choose the answer you think is best.
   New York City is the largest, so choice B is correct.
2. Find the row of dotted lines numbered the same as the question you are answering.
   This is question number 32, so find row number 32.
3. Find the pair of dotted lines corresponding to the answer you have chosen.
   You have chosen answer B, so find the pair of dotted lines marked "B".
4. Make a solid black mark between the dotted lines.
   Go up and down two or three times with your pencil so plenty of graphite rubs off, but do not let the mark get outside or above the dots.

VI. BEFORE THE TEST

Common sense will help you find procedures to follow to get ready for an examination. Too many of us, however, overlook these sensible measures. Indeed, nervousness and fatigue have been found to be the most serious reasons why applicants fail to do their best on civil service tests. Here is a list of reminders.

1. Begin Your Preparation Early

    Don't wait until the last minute to go scurrying around for books and materials or to find out what the position is all about.

2. Prepare Continuously

    An hour a night for a week is better than an all-night cram session. This has been definitely established. What is more, a night a week for a month will return better dividends than crowding your study into a shorter period of time.

3. Locate the Place of the Examination

    You have been sent a notice telling you when and where to report for the examination. If the location is in a different town or otherwise unfamiliar to you, it would be well to inquire the best route and learn something about the building.

4. Relax the Night Before the Test

    Allow your mind to rest. Do not study at all that night. Plan some mild recreation or diversion; then go to bed early and get a good night's sleep.

5. Get Up Early Enough to Make a Leisurely Trip to the Place for the Test

    Then unforeseen events, traffic snarls, unfamiliar buildings, will not upset you.

6. Dress Comfortably

    A written test is not a fashion show. You will be known by number and not by name, so wear something comfortable.

7. Leave Excess Paraphernalia at Home

    Shopping bags and odd bundles will get in your way. You need bring only the items mentioned in the official notice sent to you; usually everything you need is provided. Do not bring reference books to the examination. They will only confuse those last minutes and be taken away from you when in the test room.

8. Arrive Somewhat Ahead of Time

    If because of transportation schedules you must get there very early, bring a newspaper or magazine to take your mind off yourself while waiting.

9. Locate the Examination Room

    When you have found the proper room, you will be directed to the seat or part of the room where you will sit. Sometimes you are given a sheet of instructions to read while you are waiting. Do not fill out any forms until you are told to do so; just read them and be ready.

10. Relax and Prepare to Listen to the Instructions

11. If you have any physical problem that may keep you from doing your best, be sure to tell the test administrator. If you are sick, or in poor health, you really cannot do your best on the test. You can come back and take the test some other time.

VII. AT THE TEST

    The day of the test is here and you have the test booklet in your hand. The temptation to get going is very strong. Caution! There is more to success than knowing the right answers. You must know how to identify your papers and understand variations in the type of short-answer question used in this particular examination. Follow these suggestions for maximum results from your efforts:

1. Cooperate with the Monitor

The test administrator has a duty to create a situation in which you can be as much at ease as possible. He will give instructions, tell you when to begin, check to see that you are marking your answer sheet correctly. He is not there to guard you, although he will see that your competitors do not take unfair advantage. He wants to help you do your best.

2. Listen to All Instructions

Don't jump the gun! Wait until you understand all directions. In most civil service tests you get more time than you need to answer the questions. So don't get in a hurry. Read each word of instructions until you clearly understand the meaning. Study the examples. Listen to all announcements. Follow directions. Ask questions if you do not understand what to do.

3. Identify Your Papers

Civil service examinations are usually identified by number only. You will be assigned a number; you must not put your name on your test papers. Be sure to copy your number correctly. Since more than one examination may be given, copy your exact examination title.

4. Plan Your Time

Unless you are told that a test is a "speed" or "rate-of-work" test, speed itself is not usually important. Time enough to answer all the questions will be provided. But this does not mean that you have all day. An overall time limit has been set. Divide the total time (in minutes) by the number of questions to get the approximate time you have for each question.

5. Do Not Linger Over Difficult Questions

If you come across a difficult question, mark it with a paper clip (useful to have along) and come back to it when you have been through the booklet. One caution if you do this -- be sure to skip a number on your answer sheet too. Check often to be sure that you have not lost your place and that you are marking in the row numbered the same as the question you are answering.

6. Read the Questions

Be sure you know what the question asks! Many capable people are unsuccessful because they failed to *read* the questions correctly.

7. Answer All Questions

Unless you have been instructed that a penalty will be deducted for incorrect answers, it is better to guess than to omit a question.

8. Speed Tests

It is often better *not* to guess on speed tests. It has been found that on timed tests people are tempted to spend the last few seconds before time is called in marking answers at random -- without even reading them -- in the hope of picking up a few extra points. To discourage this practice, the instructions may warn you that your score will be "corrected" for guessing. That is, a penalty will be applied. The incorrect answers will be deducted from the correct ones, or some other penalty formula will be used.

9. Review Your Answers

If you finish before time is called, go back to the questions you guessed or omitted to give further thought to them. Review other answers if you have time.

10. Return Your Test Materials

If you are ready to leave before others have finished or time is called, take *all* your materials to the monitor and leave quietly. Never take any test material with you. The monitor can discover whose papers are not complete, and taking a test booklet may be grounds for disqualification.

VIII. EXAMINATION TECHNIQUES

1. Read the *general* instructions carefully. These are usually printed on the first page of the examination booklet. As a rule, these instructions refer to the timing of the examination; the fact that you should not start work until the signal and must stop work at a signal, etc. If there are any *special* instructions, such as a choice of questions to be answered, make sure that you note this instruction carefully.

2. When you are ready to start work on the examination, that is as soon as the signal has been given, read the instructions to each question booklet, underline any key words or phrases, such as *least*, *best*, *outline*, *describe*, and the like. In this way you will tend to answer as requested rather than discover on reviewing your paper that you *listed without describing*, that you selected the *worst* choice rather than the *best* choice, etc.

3. If the examination is of the objective or so-called multiple-choice type, that is, each question will also give a series of possible answers: A, B, C, or D, and you are called upon to select the best answer and write the letter next to that answer on your answer paper, it is advisable to start answering each question in turn. There may be anywhere from 50 to 100 such questions in the three or four hours allotted and you can see how much time would be taken if you read through all the questions before beginning to answer any. Furthermore, if you come across a question or a group of questions which you know would be difficult to answer, it would undoubtedly affect your handling of all the other questions.

4. If the examination is of the esssay-type and contains but a few questions, it is a moot point as to whether you should read all the questions before starting to answer any one. Of course if you are given a choice, say five out of seven and the like, then it is essential to read all the questions so you can eliminate the two which are most difficult. If, however, you are asked to answer all the questions, there may be danger in trying to answer the easiest one first because you may find that you will spend too much time on it. The best technique is to answer the first question, then proceed to the second, etc.

5. Time your answers. Before the examination begins, write down the time it started, then add the time allowed for the examination and write down the time it must be completed, then divide the time available somewhat as follows:

(a) If $3\frac{1}{2}$ hours are allowed, that would be 210 minutes. If you have 80 objective-type questions, that would be an average of $2\frac{1}{2}$ minutes per question. Allow yourself no more than 2 minutes per question, or a total of 160 minutes, which will permit about 50 minutes to review.

(b) If for the time allotment of 210 minutes, there are 7 essay questions to answer, that would average about 30 minutes a question. Give yourself only 25 minutes per question so that you have about 35 minutes to review.

6. The most important instruction is *to read each question* and make sure you know what is wanted. The second most important instruction is to *time yourself properly* so that you answer every question. The third most important instruction is to *answer every question*. Guess if you have to but include something for each question. Remember that you will receive no credit for a blank and will probably receive some credit if you write something in answer to an essay question. If you guess a letter, say "B" for a multiple-choice question, you may have guessed right. If you leave a blank as the answer to a multiple-choice question, the examiners may respect your feelings but it will not add a point to your score.

7. Suggestions

    a. <u>Objective-Type Questions</u>

      (1) Examine the question booklet for proper sequence of pages and questions.

      (2) Read all instructions carefully.

      (3) Skip any question which seems too difficult; return to it after all other questions have been answered.

      (4) Apportion your time properly; do not spend too much time on any single question or group of questions.

      (5) Note and underline key words -- *all, most, fewest, least, best, worst, same, opposite.*

      (6) Pay particular attention to negatives.

      (7) Note unusual option, e.g., unduly long, short, complex, different or similar in content to the body of the question.

      (8) Observe the use of "hedging" words -- *probably, may, most likely, etc.*

      (9) Make sure that your answer is put next to the same number as the question.

      (10) Do not second-guess unless you have good reason to believe the second answer is definitely more correct.

      (11) Cross out original answer if you decide another answer is more accurate; do not erase.

      (12) Answer all questions; guess unless instructed otherwise.

      (13) Leave time for review.

    b. <u>Essay-Type Questions</u>

      (1) Read each question carefully.

      (2) Determine exactly what is wanted. Underline key words or phrases.

      (3) Decide on outline or paragraph answer.

      (4) Include many different points and elements unless asked to develop any one or two points or elements.

      (5) Show impartiality by giving pros and cons unless directed to select one side only.

      (6) Make and write down any assumptions you find necessary to answer the question.

      (7) Watch your English, grammar, punctuation, choice of words.

      (8) Time your answers; don't crowd material.

8. Answering the Essay Question

    Most essay questions can be answered by framing the specific response around several key words or ideas. Here are a few such key words or ideas:

M's: manpower, materials, methods, money, management;
P's: purpose, program, policy, plan, procedure, practice,
   problems, pitfalls, personnel, public relations.

a. <u>Six Basic Steps in Handling Problems</u>:
   (1) **Pre**liminary plan and background development
   (2) Collect information, data and facts
   (3) Analyze and interpret information, data and facts
   (4) Analyze and develop solutions as well as make recommendations
   (5) Prepare report and sell recommendations
   (6) Install recommendations and follow up effectiveness

b. <u>Pitfalls to Avoid</u>
   (1) *Taking things for granted*
      A statement of the situation does not necessarily imply that each of the elements is necessarily true; for example, a complaint may be invalid and biased so that all that can be taken for granted is that a complaint has been registered.
   (2) *Considering only one side of a situation*
      Wherever possible, indicate several alternatives and then point out the reasons you selected the best one.
   (3) *Failing to indicate follow-up*
      Whenever your answer indicates action on your part, make certain that you will take proper follow-up action to see how successful your recommendations, procedures, or actions turn out to be.
   (4) *Taking too long in answering any single question*
      Remember to time your answers properly.

IX. AFTER THE TEST

Scoring procedures differ in detail among civil service jurisdictions although the general principles are the same. Whether the papers are hand-scored or graded by the electric scoring machine we have described, they are nearly always graded by number. That is, the person who marks the paper knows only the number -- never the name -- of the applicant. Not until all the papers have been graded will they be matched with names. If other tests, such as training and experience or oral interview ratings have been given, scores will be combined. Different parts of the examination usually have different weights. For example, the written test might count 60 percent of the final grade, and a rating of training and experience 40 percent. In many jurisdictions, veterans will have a certain number of points added to their grades.

After the final grade has been determined, the names are placed in grade order and an eligible list is established. There are various methods for resolving ties between those who get the same final grade: probably the most common is to place first the name of the person whose application was received first. Job offers are made from the eligible list in the order the names appear on it.

You will be notified of your grade and your rank order as soon as all these computations have been made. This will be done as rapidly as possible.

People who are found to meet the requirements in the announcement are called "eligibles." Their names are put on a list of eligibles. An eligible's chances of getting a job depend on how high he stands on this list and how fast agencies are filling jobs from the list.

When a job is to be filled from a list of eligibles, the agency asks for the names of people on the list of eligibles for that job.

When the civil service commission receives this request, it sends to the agency the names of the three people highest on the list. Or, if the job to be filled has specialized requirements, the office sends the agency, from the general list, the names of the top three persons who meet those requirements.

The appointing officer makes a **choice from among** the three people whose names were sent to him. If **the selected person** accepts the appointment, the names of the others **are put back** on the list to be considered for future openings.

That is the rule in hiring from all kinds of eligible lists, whether they are for typist, carpenter, chemist, or something else. For every vacancy, the appointing officer has his choice of any one of the top three eligibles on the list. This explains why the person whose name is on top of the list sometimes does not get an appointment when some of the persons lower on the list do. If the appointing officer chooses the No.2 or No.3 eligible, the No.1 eligible does not get a job at once, but stays on the list until he is appointed or the list is terminated.

X. HOW TO PASS THE INTERVIEW TEST

The examination for which you applied requires an oral interview test. You have already taken the written test and you are now being called for the interview test -- the final part of the formal examination.

You may think that it is not possible to prepare for an interview test and that there are no procedures to follow during an interview.

Our purpose is to point out some things you can do in advance that will help you and some good rules to follow and pitfalls to avoid while you are being interviewed.

A. *WHAT IS AN INTERVIEW SUPPOSED TO TEST?*

The written examination is designed to test the technical knowledge and competence of the candidate; the oral is designed to evaluate intangible qualities, not readily measured otherwise, and to establish a list showing the relative fitness of each candidate, *as measured against his competitors,* for the position sought. Scoring is not on the basis of "right" or "wrong," but on a sliding scale of values ranging from "not passable" to "outstanding." As a matter of fact, it is possible to achieve a relatively low score without a single "incorrect" answer because of evident weakness in the qualities being measured,

Occasionally, an examination may consist entirely of an oral test -- either an individual or a group oral. In such cases, information is sought concerning the technical knowledges and abilities of the candidate, since there has been no written examination for this purpose. More commonly, however, an oral test is used to supplement a written examination.

B. *WHO CONDUCTS INTERVIEWS?*

The composition of oral boards varies among different jurisdictions. **In nearly all,** a representative of the personnel department **serves as chairman.** One of the members of the board may be a representative of the **d**epartment in which the candidate would work. In **some cases,** "outside experts" are used, and, frequently, a business **man or some** other representative of the general public is asked to serve. Labor and management or other special groups may be represented. The aim is to secure the services of experts in the appropriate field.

However the board is composed, it is a good idea (and not at all improper or unethical) to ascertain in advance of the interview who the members are and what groups they represent. When you are introduced to them, you will have some idea of their backgrounds and interests, and at least you will not stutter and stammer over their names.

C. *WHAT TO DO BEFORE THE INTERVIEW*

While knowledge about the board members is useful and takes some of the surprise element out of the interview, there is other preparation which is more substantive. It *is* possible to prepare for an oral -- in several ways:

1. Keep a Copy of Your Application and Review it Carefully Before the Interview

    This may be the only document before the oral board, and the starting point of the interview. Know what experience and education you have listed there, and the sequence and dates of it. Sometimes the board will ask *you* to review the highlights of your experience for them; you should not have to hem and haw doing it.

2. Study the Class Specification and the Examination Announcement

    Usually, the oral board has one or both of these to guide them. The qualities, characteristics, or knowledges required by the position sought are stated in these documents. They offer valuable clues as to the nature of the oral interview. For example, if the job involves supervisory responsibilities, the announcement will usually indicate that knowledge of modern supervisory methods and the qualifications of the candidate as a supervisor will be tested. If so, you can expect such questions, frequently in the form of a hypothetical situation which you are expected to solve. *Never* go into an oral without knowledge of the duties and responsibilities of the job you seek.

3. Think Through Each Qualification Required

    Try to visualize the kind of questions *you* would ask if you were a board member. How well could you answer them? Try especially to appraise your own knowledge and background in each area, *measured against the job sought,* and identify any areas in which you are weak. Be critical and realistic -- do not flatter yourself.

4. Do Some General Reading in Areas in Which You Feel You May be Weak

    For example, if the job involves supervision and your past experience has *not,* some general reading in supervisory methods and practices, particularly in the field of human relations, might be useful. *Do not* study agency procedures or detailed manuals. The oral board will be testing your understanding and capacity, *not* your memory.

5. Get a Good Night's Sleep and Watch Your General Health and Mental Attitude

    You will want a clear head at the interview. Take care of a cold or other minor ailment, and, of course, *no hangovers.*

D. *WHAT TO DO THE DAY OF THE INTERVIEW*

Now comes the day of the interview itself. Give yourself plenty of time to get there. Plan to arrive somewhat ahead of the scheduled time, particularly if your appointment is in the fore part of the day. If a previous candidate fails to appear, the board might be ready for you a bit early. By early afternoon an oral board is almost invariably behind schedule if there are many candidates, and you may have to wait. Take along a book or magazine to read, or your application to review. But leave any extraneous material in the waiting room when you go in for your interview. In any event, relax and compose yourself.

The matter of dress is important. The board is forming impressions about you -- from your experience, your manners, your attitudes, and from your appearance. Give your personal appearance careful attention. Dress your *best*, but not your flashiest. Choose conservative, appropriate clothing, and be sure it and you are immaculate. This is a business interview, and your appearance should indicate that you regard it as such. Besides, being well-groomed and properly dressed will help boost your confidence.

Sooner or later, someone will call your name and escort you into the interview room. *This is it.* From here on you are on your own. It is too late for any more preparation. But, remember, you asked for this opportunity to prove your fitness, and you are here because your request was granted.

E. *WHAT HAPPENS WHEN YOU GO IN?*

The usual sequence of events will be as follows: The clerk (who is often the board stenographer) will introduce you to the chairman of the oral board, who will introduce you to each other member of the board. Acknowledge the introductions before you sit down. Do not be surprised if you find a microphone facing you or a stenotypist sitting by. Oral interviews are usually recorded, in the event of an appeal or other review.

Usually the chairman of the board will open the interview by reviewing the highlights of your education and work experience from your application -- primarily for the benefit of the other members of the board, as well as to get the material into the record. Do not interrupt or comment unless there is an error or significant misinterpretation; if so, do not hesitate. But do not quibble about insignificant matters. Usually, also, he will ask you some question about your education, your experience, or your present job -- partly to get you started talking, to establish the interviewing "rapport." He may start the actual questioning, or turn it over to one of the other members. Frequently each member undertakes the questioning on a particular area, one in which he is perhaps most competent. So you can expect each member to participate in the examination. And because the time is limited, you may expect some rather abrupt switches in the direction the questioning takes. Do not be upset by it. Normally, a board member will not pursue a single line of questioning unless he discovers a particular strength or weakness.

After each member has participated, the chairman will usually ask whether any member has any further questions, then will ask you if you have anything you wish to add. Unless you are expecting this question, it may floor you. Or worse, it may start you off on an extended, extemporaneous speech. The board is not usually seeking more information. The question is principally to offer you a last opportunity to present further qualifications or to indicate that you have nothing to add. So, if you feel that a significant qualification or characteristic has been overlooked, it is proper to point it out in a sentence or so. Do not compliment the board on the thoroughness of their examination -- they have been sketchy, and you know it. If you wish, merely say, "No thank you, I have nothing further to add." This is a point where you can "talk yourself out" of a good impression or fail to present an important bit of information. *Remember, you close the interview yourself.*

The chairman will then say,"That is all,Mr.Smith,thank you." Do not be startled; the interview is over, and quicker than you think. Say,"Thank you and good morning," gather up your belongings and take your leave. Save your sigh of relief for the other side of the door.

F. HOW TO PUT YOUR BEST FOOT FORWARD

Throughout all this process, you may feel that the board individually and collectively is trying to pierce your defenses, to seek out your hidden weaknesses, and to embarrass and confuse you. Actually, this is not true. They are obliged to make an appraisal of your qualifications for the job you are seeking, and they *want to see you in your best light*. Remember, they must interview all candidates and a noncooperative candidate may become a failure in spite of their best efforts to bring out his qualifications. Here are fifteen(15) suggestions that will help you:

1. <u>Be Natural. Keep Your Attitude Confident,But Not Cocky</u>

If *you* are not confident that you can do the job, do not ex-expect the *board* to be. Do not apologize for your weaknesses, try to bring out your strong points. The board is interested in a positive, not a negative presentation. Cockiness will antagonize any board member, and make him wonder if you are covering up a weakness by a false show of strength.

2. <u>Get Comfortable, But Don't Lounge or Sprawl</u>

Sit erectly but not stiffly. A careless posture may lead the board to conclude you are careless in other things, or at least that you are not impressed by the importance of the occasion to you.Either conclusion is natural, even if incorrect. Do not fuss with your clothing, or with a pencil or an ashtray. Your hands may occasionally be useful to emphasize a point; do not let them become a point of distraction.

3. <u>Do Not Wisecrack or Make Small Talk</u>

This is a serious situation, and your attitude should show that you consider it as such. Further, the time of the board is limited; they do not want to waste it, and neither should you.

4. <u>Do Not Exaggerate Your Experience or Abilities</u>

In the first place, from information in the application,from other interviews and other sources, the board may know more about you than you think; in the second place, you probably will not get away with it in the first place. An experienced board is rather adept at spotting such a situation. Do not take the chance.

5. <u>If You Know a Member of the Board, Do Not Make a Point of It</u>, <u>Yet Do Not Hide It.</u>

Certainly you are not fooling him, and probably not the other members of the board. Do not try to take advantage of your acquaintanceship -- it will probably do you little good.

6. <u>Do Not Dominate the Interview</u>

Let the board do that. They will give you the clues -- do not assume that you have to do all the talking. Realize that the board has a number of questions to ask you, and do not try to take up all the interview time by showing off your extensive knowledge of the answer to the first one.

7. Be Attentive

You only have twenty minutes or so, and you should keep your attention at its sharpest throughout. When a member is addressing a problem or a question to you, give him your undivided attention. Address your reply principally to him, but do not exclude the other members of the board.

8. Do Not Interrupt

A board member may be stating a problem for you to analyze. He will ask you a question when the time comes. Let him state the problem, and wait for the question.

9. Make Sure You Understand the Question

Do not try to answer until you are sure what the question is. If it is not clear, restate it in your own words or ask the board member to clarify it for you. But do not haggle about minor elements.

10. Reply Promptly But Not Hastily

A common entry on oral board rating sheets is "candidate responded readily," or "candidate hesitated in replies." Respond as promptly and quickly as you can, but do not jump to a hasty, ill-considered answer.

11. Do Not Be Peremptory in Your Answers

A brief answer is proper -- but do not fire your answer back. That is a losing game from your point of view. The board member can probably ask questions much faster than you can answer them.

12. Do Not Try To Create the Answer You Think the Board Member Wants

He is interested in what kind of mind you have and how it works -- not in playing games. Furthermore, he can usually spot this practice and will usually grade you down on it.

13. Do Not Switch Sides in Your Reply Merely to Agree With a Board Member

Frequently, a member will take a contrary position merely to draw you out and to see if you are willing and able to defend your point of view. Do not start a debate, yet do not surrender a good position. If a position is worth taking, it is worth defending.

14. Do Not Be Afraid to Admit an Error in Judgment if You Are Shown to Be Wrong

The board knows that you are forced to reply without any opportunity for careful consideration. Your answer may be demonstrably wrong. If so, admit it and get on with the interview.

15. Do Not Dwell at Length on Your Present Job

The opening question may relate to your present assignment. Answer the question but do not go into an extended discussion. You are being examined for a *new* job, not your present one. As a matter of fact, try to phrase *all* your answers in terms of the job for which you are being examined.

G. BASIS OF RATING

Probably you will forget most of these "do's" and "don'ts" when you walk into the oral interview room. Even remembering them all will not insure you a passing grade. Perhaps you did not have the qualifications in the first place. But remembering them *will* help you to put your best foot forward, without treading on the toes of the board members.

Rumor and popular opinion to the contrary notwithstanding, an oral board wants you to make the best appearance possible. They know you are under pressure -- but they also want to see how you respond to it as a guide to what your reaction would be under the pressures of the job you seek. They will be influenced by the degree of poise you display, the personal traits you show, and the manner in which you respond.

EXAMINATION SECTION

EXAMINATION SECTION
TEST 1

DIRECTIONS: Each question or incomplete statement is followed by several suggested answers or completions. Select the one that BEST answers the question or completes the statement. *PRINT THE LETTER OF THE CORRECT ANSWER IN THE SPACE AT THE RIGHT.*

1. The speed disparity between adjacent devices can cause problems with an interface.
   These problems are usually resolved by temporarily storing input in a(n)
   A. channel   B. control unit
   C. register   D. buffer   1.___

2. A typical computer spends most of its time   2.___
   A. compiling
   B. waiting for input or output
   C. executing instructions
   D. interpreting commands

3. What is the basic input device on a small computer?   3.___
   A. Keyboard   B. Cursor   C. Mouse   D. Processor

4. When two hardware devices want to communicate, they will   4.___
   FIRST exchange _____ signals.
   A. interrupt B. protocol   C. interface D. boot

5. Which of the following is retrieved and executed by the   5.___
   processor?
   A. Instructions   B. Clock pulses
   C. Information   D. Data

6. What type of architecture is used by most microcomputers?   6.___
   A. Standard   B. Serial
   C. Single-bus   D. Multiple-bus

7. Typically, _____ is NOT a problem associated with a   7.___
   computer's main memory.
   A. cost   B. volatility
   C. capacity   D. speed

8. Which of the following types of memory management is the   8.___
   SIMPLEST?
   A. Sector-oriented   B. Dynamic
   C. Block-oriented   D. Fixed partition

9. What is the term for the time during which a disk drive   9.___
   is brought up to operating speed and the access device is
   positioned?
   A. E-time   B. Rotational delay
   C. Seek time   D. Access time

10. What type of code is written by programmers?   10.___
    A. Load module   B. Source
    C. Object   D. Operating

11. A _____ is the basic output device on a small computer.   11.___
    A. printer   B. keyboard
    C. display screen   D. hard disk

12. Which of the following serves to manage a computer's   12.___
    resources?
    A. User   B. Operating system
    C. Programmer   D. Software

13. A computer processes data into   13.___
    A. information   B. pulses
    C. code   D. facts

14. What is the term for the entity used to link external   14.___
    devices to a small computer system?
    A. Interface   B. Network
    C. Plug-in   D. Modem

15. For a transaction processing application, a _____ file   15.___
    organization should be selected.
    A. sequential   B. indexed
    C. direct   D. random

16. Which element of a microcomputer directly controls input   16.___
    and output?
    A. Buffer   B. Processor
    C. Bus   D. Control unit

17. A computer's data and program instructions are stored in   17.___
    A. memory   B. the video buffer
    C. a program   D. an output port

18. What is the term for the metal framework around which   18.___
    most microcomputers are constructed?
    A. Mainframe   B. Hard disk
    C. Motherboard   D. Expansion slot

19. The read/write head of a computer's disk drive is   19.___
    contained on the
    A. magnetic drum   B. data element
    C. token   D. access mechanism

20. A(n) _____ is used to link a small computer's secondary   20.___
    storage device to the system.
    A. control unit   B. interface board
    C. register   D. buffer

21. What processor management technique is used on most time-   21.___
    sharing network systems?
    A. Time-slicing   B. Command sorting
    C. Apportionment   D. Interrupt processing

22. Which of the following procedures is used to copy data   22.___
    from a slow-speed device to a high-speed device for
    eventual input to a program?
    A. Queuing   B. Spooling
    C. Buffing   D. Scheduling

23. A location in memory is located by its   23.___
    A. section   B. register   C. address   D. decoder

24. _____ data is represented by a wave.   24.___
    A. Microwave B. Digital   C. Binary   D. Analog

25. A programmer defines the logical structure of a problem   25.___
    by using a(n)
    A. assembler   B. compiler
    C. interpreter   D. nonprocedural language

KEY (CORRECT ANSWERS)

1. D		11. C	
2. B		12. B	
3. A		13. A	
4. B		14. A	
5. A		15. C	
6. C		16. B	
7. D		17. A	
8. D		18. C	
9. C		19. D	
10. B		20. B	

21. A
22. B
23. C
24. D
25. D

TEST 2

DIRECTIONS: Each question or incomplete statement is followed by several suggested answers or completions. Select the one that BEST answers the question or completes the statement. *PRINT THE LETTER OF THE CORRECT ANSWER IN THE SPACE AT THE RIGHT.*

1. Data is converted from digital to analog form through the process of
   A. demodulation
   B. teleporting
   C. cross-modulation
   D. modulation

   1.___

2. Which of the following represents the simplest data structure?
   A. Record   B. File   C. List   D. Directory

   2.___

3. The term for a set of parallel wires used to transmit data, commands, or power is
   A. bus
   B. cabling
   C. line
   D. twisted pair

   3.___

4. _____ limit the number of peripherals that can be linked to a microcomputer system.
   A. Channels
   B. Bus lines
   C. Buffers
   D. Slots

   4.___

5. A data structure in which memory is allocated as a series of numbered cells is a(n)
   A. array   B. block   C. record   D. register

   5.___

6. On a disk, each program's name and location can be located on the
   A. index   B. address   C. label   D. register

   6.___

7. Onto which of the following structures is a processing chip stored?
   A. Board   B. Plate   C. Bus   D. Disk

   7.___

8. Two or more independent processors can share the same memory under a system known as
   A. time-sharing
   B. FAT binaries
   C. multitasking
   D. multiprocessing

   8.___

9. A _____ is the basic storage unit around which a micro-computer system is designed.
   A. bit   B. block   C. word   D. byte

   9.___

10. A user communicates with an operating system by means of a(n)
    A. interface
    B. peripheral
    C. command language
    D. application

    10.___

11. A _____ is used to convert data from pulse form to wave   11.___
    form and back again.
    A. channel   B. modem   C. SCSI port   D. bus

12. Data values can be accessed according to their element   12.___
    numbers in a(n)
    A. list   B. register   C. record   D. array

13. Under a _____ memory management scheme, a program is   13.___
    allocated as much memory as it needs.
    A. sector-oriented   B. dynamic
    C. block-oriented   D. fixed partition

14. What is the term for the process of removing errors from   14.___
    a program?
    A. Compiling   B. Debugging
    C. Troubleshooting   D. Extraction

15. _____ is the term for the time during which a desired   15.___
    sector of a disk approaches the access device.
    A. Run time   B. Rotational delay
    C. Seek time   D. Access time

16. What is the term for the process by which a networked   16.___
    computer selects the terminal it will communicate with?
    A. Compiling   B. Polling
    C. Interfacing   D. Selection

17. After compilers and assemblers read a programmer's code,   17.___
    they generate a(n)
    A. object module   B. nonprocedural language
    C. subroutine   D. load module

18. Memory that loses its content when the machine's power   18.___
    is turned off is described as
    A. read-only   B. redundant
    C. dependent   D. volatile

19. Which module of an operating system sends primitive   19.___
    commands to a disk drive?
    A. Motherboard   B. IOCS
    C. CPU   D. Command processor

20. The BASIC measure of data communications speed is   20.___
    A. bit rate   B. baud rate
    C. kilobytes per second   D. bits per second

21. The term _____ is used to denote a single, meaningful   21.___
    data element, such as a person's telephone number.
    A. field   B. item   C. record   D. file

22. What is the term for the machine-level translation of a   22.___
    programmer's source code?
    A. Load module   B. Subroutine
    C. Source library   D. Object module

23. Which part of an instruction directs the actions of the   23.___
processor?
   A. Pulse   B. Operation code
   C. Statement   D. Operand

24. A _____ is used to store programs that enter a multi-   24.___
programming system.
   A. tape   B. spool   C. buffer   D. queue

25. _____ is a device used to avoid data dependency and   25.___
redundancy.
   A. Sequential filing   B. Continuous backup
   C. Random filing   D. Database

KEY (CORRECT ANSWERS)

1. A	11. B		
2. C	12. D		
3. A	13. B		
4. D	14. B		
5. A	15. B		
6. A	16. B		
7. A	17. A		
8. D	18. D		
9. C	19. B		
10. C	20. B		

21. A
22. D
23. B
24. D
25. D

EXAMINATION SECTION
TEST 1

DIRECTIONS: Each question or incomplete statement is followed by several suggested answers or completions. Select the one that BEST answers the question or completes the statement. *PRINT THE LETTER OF THE CORRECT ANSWER IN THE SPACE AT THE RIGHT.*

1. A track and a sector number on a disk combine to form a(n) 1.___
   A. register   B. byte   C. address   D. file name

2. A(n) _____ microcomputer system design focuses on what 2.___
   must be done, but not on how to do it.
   A. logical   B. listed   C. protocol   D. objective

3. An instruction is retrieved from main memory by the _____ 3.___
   processor component.
   A. arithmetic and logic unit
   B. instruction counter
   C. register
   D. instruction control unit

4. What is the term for a support program that reads a 4.___
   source program, translates the source statements to
   machine language, and outputs a complete binary object
   program?
   A. Scheduler   B. Interpreter
   C. Compiler   D. Assembler

5. A(n) _____ is composed of a group of related data records. 5.___
   A. array   B. list   C. directory   D. file

6. What is the term for an extra bit added to data bits that 6.___
   will allow a computer to check the bit pattern for
   accuracy?
   A. End code   B. Bit stuffer
   C. Operand   D. Parity bit

7. When disks are stacked into a pack, what is the term for 7.___
   the set of tracks accessed by the access device?
   A. Block   B. Sector   C. Cylinder   D. Drum

8. Any data communications medium can be described by the 8.___
   generic term
   A. line   B. port   C. converter   D. modem

9. The operating systems of most microcomputers are driven by 9.___
   A. commands   B. hardware
   C. software   D. a control unit

10. What is the term for a complete machine-level program   10.___
    that is in a form ready to be placed into main memory
    and executed?
    A. Load module   B. Object module
    C. Schedule   D. Compiler

11. A programmer writes one instruction for each machine-   11.___
    level instruction when using a(n)
    A. generator   B. assembler
    C. resource fork   D. compiler

12. A binary digit is represented by a   12.___
    A. byte   B. code   C. bit   D. buffer

13. Which module of the operating system is responsible for   13.___
    communicating with input and output devices?
    A. Command processor   B. Boot
    C. IOCS   D. Bus line

14. Two or more disks stacked on a common drive shaft are   14.___
    known as a
    A. pack   B. roll-out
    C. multidrive   D. cylinder

15. The _____ of an operating system loads programs into main   15.___
    memory.
    A. compiler   B. processor manager
    C. scheduler   D. assembler

16. A _____ can be used to synchronize devices or media that   16.___
    operate at different speeds.
    A. buffer   B. spooler   C. modem   D. protocol

17. The part of an instruction that identifies memory   17.___
    locations to participate in an operation is the
    A. pulse   B. statement
    C. operand   D. operation code

18. What is the term for a support program that reads a   18.___
    single source statement, translates the statement to
    machine language, executes the instructions, and then
    moves onto the next source statement?
    A. Scheduler   B. Interpreter
    C. Compiler   D. Assembler

19. _____ is used to link a computer's internal components. 19.___
    A. Cables   B. Bus lines
    C. Clock pulses   D. Motherboard

20. Data are transferred from main memory to a disk's surface 20.___
    in units called
    A. sectors   B. blocks   C. tracks   D. words

21. Under a _____ memory management scheme, programs are   21.___
    stored on disk, with only active portions stored into
    memory.
    A. virtual   B. dynamic
    C. block-oriented   D. fixed partition

22. A(n) _____ is composed of a group of related data fields.   22.___
    A. array   B. list   C. record   D. file

23. Which of the following serves to allocate a processor's   23.___
    time?
    A. User   B. Bus
    C. Operating system   D. Motherboard

24. On a disk, the address of the beginning of each program   24.___
    is stored on the
    A. tree   B. block   C. index   D. register

25. A program's steps are divided into units of   25.___
    A. code   B. commands
    C. sectors   D. instructions

———

KEY (CORRECT ANSWERS)

1. C		11. B	
2. A		12. C	
3. D		13. C	
4. C		14. A	
5. D		15. C	
6. D		16. A	
7. C		17. C	
8. A		18. B	
9. A		19. B	
10. A		20. A	

21. A
22. C
23. C
24. C
25. D

———

TEST 2

DIRECTIONS: Each question or incomplete statement is followed by
several suggested answers or completions. Select the
one that BEST answers the question or completes the
statement. *PRINT THE LETTER OF THE CORRECT ANSWER IN
THE SPACE AT THE RIGHT.*

1. The address of the next instruction to be executed is held   1.___
    in the _____ processor component.
    A. main memory
    B. register
    C. arithmetic and logic unit
    D. instruction control unit

2. What is the term for an electronic signal that is part of   2.___
    a protocol?
    A. Token   B. Reach   C. Chord   D. Pulse

3. Under _____ processing, data records are processed in the   3.___
    order in which they are recorded.
    A. continuous   B. consecutive
    C. serial   D. sequential

4. _____ processing is a computer application in which data   4.___
    are collected over time and then processed together.
    A. Transaction   B. Cumulative
    C. Batch   D. Continuous

5. A(n) _____ serves as a hardware/software interface.   5.___
    A. buffer   B. application
    C. operating system   D. bus

6. Any connection for an electronic communication line can   6.___
    be called a(n)
    A. port   B. poll   C. line   D. front end

7. During a single machine cycle, a processor retrieves and   7.___
    executes
    A. one command
    B. one instruction
    C. at least two statements
    D. at least two instructions

8. A _____ is NOT an example of a data structure.   8.___
    A. record   B. file   C. list   D. directory

9. Which of the following serves to translate a computer's   9.___
    internal codes and a peripheral device's external codes?
    A. Buffer   B. RAM
    C. Interface   D. Encoder/decoder

10. Which of the following is the memory management scheme
    MOST often used with time-shared systems?   10.___
    A. Pages   B. Roll-in/roll-out
    C. Fixed partitions   D. First-come/first-serve

11. When the same data are recorded in two or more files,   11.___
    _____ has occurred.
    A. redundancy   B. leakage
    C. backup   D. loss

12. For a batch processing application, a _____ file   12.___
    organization should be selected.
    A. sequential   B. indexed
    C. direct   D. random

13. If a bus line transmits bits one by one, it is described   13.___
    as a _____ line.
    A. serial   B. consecutive
    C. continuous   D. parallel

14. Data is converted from analog to digital form through   14.___
    the process of
    A. demodulation   B. data flow
    C. cross-modulation   D. modulation

15. A _____ loads a computer's operating system.   15.___
    A. program loader   B. IOCS
    C. command processor   D. boot

16. Which of the following differentiates a computer from a   16.___
    calculator?
    A. Memory   B. Input
    C. A processor   D. A stored program

17. Which element of a microcomputer system will devote a   17.___
    separate unit to suit each peripheral?
    A. Bus   B. Channel
    C. Motherboard   D. Interface

18. What is the term for the interference that distorts   18.___
    electronic signals transmitted over a distance?
    A. Ghosting   B. Noise
    C. Static   D. Interference

19. By responding to a(n) _____, an operating system can   19.___
    switch from program to program.
    A. operand   B. user
    C. interrupter   D. program

20. If a microcomputer system's memory capacity is adjusted,   20.___
    the result will be a change in
    A. word size   B. processing speed
    C. precision   D. seek time

21. A _____ generates the regular electronic pulses that drive   21.___
    a computer.
    A. clock   B. IOCS   C. bus   D. processor

22. Under what type of access can data records be accessed   22.___
    in any order?
    A. Serial   B. Random
    C. Direct   D. Sequential

23. A _____ is a brief message printed or displayed by a   23.___
    program or the operating system that asks the user for
    input.
    A. token   B. seek   C. protocol   D. prompt

24. Data on a disk are recorded in a series of concentric   24.___
    circles called
    A. blocks   B. tracks   C. cycles   D. sectors

25. What is the term for a programming language in which one   25.___
    mnemonic source statement is coded for each machine-
    level instruction?
    A. Scheduler   B. Interpreter
    C. Compiler   D. Assembler

KEY (CORRECT ANSWERS)

1. B	11. A
2. A	12. A
3. D	13. A
4. C	14. D
5. C	15. D
6. A	16. D
7. B	17. D
8. D	18. B
9. C	19. C
10. B	20. B

21. A
22. C
23. D
24. B
25. D

EXAMINATION SECTION
TEST 1

DIRECTIONS: Each question or incomplete statement is followed by several suggested answers or completions. Select the one that BEST answers the question or completes the statement. *PRINT THE LETTER OF THE CORRECT ANSWER IN THE SPACE AT THE RIGHT.*

1. A spreadsheet program is NOT used for
   A. determining averages   B. scheduling
   C. writing reports   D. estimating job costs

   1.___

2. In order to write-protect a 3.5" floppy disk, a user must
   A. cover the write-protect notch
   B. move the write-protect tab down, leaving an opening in the corner of the disk
   C. cover the recording window
   D. immobilize the shutter mechanism

   2.___

3. Which of the following is a mathematical function of a spreadsheet program?
   A. Averages   B. Logarithms
   C. Standard deviation   D. Maximum/minimum values

   3.___

4. The purpose of a device driver is to
   A. tell hardware devices precisely how to perform their jobs
   B. manage the movement of a read/write head over a hard disk drive
   C. facilitate the I/O interface
   D. manage the movement of a read/write head over a floppy disk

   4.___

5. Each of the following is a purpose that is typically served with a desktop publishing program EXCEPT
   A. printing newsletters   B. illustrating manuals
   C. creating flyers   D. printing menus

   5.___

6. Which of the following is an operating system that relies on icon selection or menu options to select commands?
   A. OS/2   B. Unix   C. MS-DOS   D. Windows

   6.___

7. Typically, the quality of a printer is expressed in terms of
   A. resolution   B. RAM
   C. DPI   D. pixellation

   7.___

8. Which of the following is a purpose that can be served by a database program?
   A. Balancing accounts
   B. Illustrating manuals
   C. Keeping track of schedules
   D. Generating client reports

   8.___

9. What type of adapter would be required if a user wanted to upgrade the graphics capability of a computer monitor to a maximum number of 256 possible colors?

    A. XGA   B. CGA   C. VGA   D. SVGS

9.___

10. Which of the following is a statistical function of a spreadsheet program?

    A. Maximum/minimum values   B. Logarithms
    C. Absolute values   D. Compounding periods

10.___

11. For which of the following functions would a flat-file database be MOST useful?

    A. Compiling invoices
    B. Creating a graph based on stored sales figures
    C. Storing information to print mailing labels
    D. Calculating inventory

11.___

12. Data in electronic spreadsheets are stored in areas called

    A. records   B. cells   C. plug-ins   D. fields

12.___

13. If a user on a network wants to receive information from a host computer, he/she would have to _____ the desired files.

    A. uplink   B. translate
    C. write a call program for D. download

13.___

14. A _____ is an optical storage device.

    A. video buffer   B. floppy disk
    C. CD-ROM   D. magnetic tape

14.___

15. Each of the following is a function served by a utility program EXCEPT

    A. removing viruses   B. setting alarms
    C. creating reports   D. creating menus

15.___

Questions 16-25.

DIRECTIONS: Questions 16 through 25 concern the DOS command-driven environment. For the purpose stated next to each number, choose the command that would need to be typed next to the prompt on a user's computer screen.

16. To find out what's stored on a disk, type

    A. ver   B. dir   C. list   D. cd

16.___

17. To clear the display screen, type

    A. ren   B. chkdsk   C. clear   D. cls

17.___

18. To create a directory or subdirectory, type

    A. md   B. rd   C. ren   D. new

18.___

19. To display the version number of the installed DOS, type   19.___
    A. type   B. DOStype   C. format   D. ver

20. To delete a directory or subdirectory, type   20.___
    A. del   B. md   C. rd   D. delete

21. To prepare a hard disk for formatting, type   21.___
    A. format   B. fdisk   C. chkdisk   D. rd

22. To list the contents of an ASCII file on screen, type   22.___
    A. file   B. list   C. type   D. asc

23. To copy a file or a directory, type   23.___
    A. xcopy   B. file/dir
    C. copy   D. diskcopy

24. To rename a file, type   24.___
    A. name   B. cd   C. rest   D. ren

25. To delete a directory, type   25.___
    A. rmdir   B. cd   C. del   D. deldir

———

KEY (CORRECT ANSWERS)

1. C		11. C	
2. B		12. B	
3. B		13. D	
4. A		14. C	
5. B		15. C	
6. A		16. B	
7. C		17. D	
8. D		18. A	
9. D		19. D	
10. A		20. C	

21. B
22. C
23. A
24. D
25. A

———

TEST 2

DIRECTIONS: Each question or incomplete statement is followed by several suggested answers or completions. Select the one that BEST answers the question or completes the statement. *PRINT THE LETTER OF THE CORRECT ANSWER IN THE SPACE AT THE RIGHT.*

Questions 1-25 concern Macintosh applications.

1. Mac users can find the amount of space available on a disk   1.___
   A. in the upper right corner of the disk window
   B. by consulting the System file
   C. by keying command-M
   D. only by using the Get Info command under a File menu

2. The simplest way for a user to make a copy of a file into   2.___
   another folder on the same disk is to
   A. select the file, then choose *Duplicate* from the file menu
   B. hold down the option key as the file is dragged into the folder
   C. select the file and press Command D
   D. make a copy onto a floppy disk and then drag that copy back onto the hard disk

3. When a user drags a file from the hard disk to a floppy   3.___
   disk, the user is
   A. moving the file from the hard disk to the floppy disk
   B. making a copy of the file for the hard disk
   C. making a copy of the file onto the floppy disk
   D. deleting the file

4. When printing to a new printer for the first time, which   4.___
   of the following should be performed FIRST?
   A. Choose the printer driver
   B. Choose the name of the printer
   C. Select *Chooser* from the Apple or File menu
   D. Click the setup button or choose Auto Setup

5. When using a mouse to select an icon, which of the   5.___
   following actions is necessary?
   A. Single-click   B. Double-click
   C. Press   D. Press and drag

6. When using a mouse to see what's in a menu, which of the   6.___
   following actions is necessary?
   A. Single-click   B. Double-click
   C. Press   D. Press and drag

7. When using a mouse to open a file, you should   7.___
   A. single-click   B. double-click
   C. press   D. press and drag

8. What is the keyboard shortcut for closing a window   8.___
   displayed on the desktop?
   A. Command W   B. Control Option E
   C. Command C   D. Command O

9. When the *Save As...* dialog box is on the desktop, what is   9.___
   the visual cue that the displayed list has been selected?
   A. All file names appear in gray
   B. A flashing insertion point
   C. Folder names appear in black
   D. A double border around the list

10. In any text environment, pressing the delete key will   10.___
    cause the _____ to back up a space.
    A. finder   B. I-beam
    C. insertion point   D. pointer

11. What is the keyboard shortcut for pasting text?   11.___
    Command
    A. V   B. X   C. B   D. C

12. Which control panel would be used to change the size of   12.___
    the type of the windows on the Desktop?
    A. General Controls   B. Views
    C. Monitors   D. Labels

13. Which control panel would be adjusted to display fewer   13.___
    colors on the monitor in order to save memory?
    A. ColorSync B. Views   C. Monitors   D. Colors

14. If a real file is thrown away by a user, its aliases will   14.___
    A. remain unaffected
    B. be deleted also
    C. remain but may only provide access to text files
    D. remain on the disk but will not provide access to
       anything

15. In any set of buttons on the desktop, the default button   15.___
    will
    A. be bordered in gray
    B. be lettered in gray
    C. have a thick double border
    D. be lettered in black

16. Whenever a menu item is followed by an ellipsis (...),   16.___
    the selection of that item will produce a(n)
    A. opened file
    B. dialog box
    C. opened application
    D. choice among listed Control Panels

17. When a set of options appear with checkbox buttons next   17.___
to them, this is a clue that
    A. a submenu will be produced by clicking a button
    B. any number of buttons may be selected or deselected
       in combination
    C. clicking a button will not produce any changes until
       the computer is restarted
    D. only one of the buttons may be selected at a time

18. If a disk's, folder's, or application's icon appears gray,   18.___
it is a sign that the item
    A. the application that created it cannot be found
    B. is about to have its name changed
    C. is already open
    D. has been deleted from the RAM

19. If a document icon is blank, it is probably a sign that   19.___
    A. it has already been opened
    B. the application that created it has already been
      opened
    C. it has been deleted
    D. the application that created the document cannot be
      found on the disk

20. If a scroll bar in a window or dialog box appears gray,   20.___
it is a sign that
    A. there are other items in the window that are not
      currently visible
    B. the display needs vertical centering
    C. the scroll box is not available
    D. the display needs horizontal centering

21. What is the keyboard shortcut for creating a new folder?   21.___
    A. Command W   B. Command F
    C. Command N   D. Control Option F

22. What is the visual clue that the name of a file, folder,   22.___
or disk on the desktop is about to be changed?
    A. A border has appeared around the name.
    B. The entire icon is highlighted.
    C. The name is highlighted.
    D. The entire icon is gray.

23. To print the contents of an entire screen, a user should   23.___
    A. choose *Print* from the file menu while running an
      application
    B. choose *Print Desktop* from the file menu
    C. press Command P
    D. choose *Print Window* from the file menu

24. When the *Save As*... dialog box is on the desktop, what   24.___
    should a user do to select the edit box for input?
    A. Press the Tab key
    B. Click on the *save* button
    C. Press the Shift key
    D. Press Command S

25. To put files back where they came from, a user should   25.___
    A. drag the file into the System folder while the *Fast
       Find* Apple menu is running
    B. press Command W
    C. create an alias
    D. press Command Y

———

KEY (CORRECT ANSWERS)

1. A		11. A	
2. B		12. B	
3. C		13. C	
4. C		14. D	
5. A		15. C	
6. C		16. B	
7. B		17. B	
8. A		18. C	
9. D		19. D	
10. C		20. A	

21. C
22. A
23. B
24. A
25. D

———

EXAMINATION SECTION

TEST 1

DIRECTIONS: Each question or incomplete statement is followed by several suggested answers or completions. Select the one that BEST answers the question or completes the statement. *PRINT THE LETTER OF THE CORRECT ANSWER IN THE SPACE AT THE RIGHT.*

1. The maintenance and use of computer hardware is assigned to the ____ group in the data processing department.
   A. systems   B. programming   C. database
   D. analysis   E. operations   1.___

2. The equipment which makes up a computer system is called
   A. hardcopy   B. software
   C. CPU   D. peripheral devices
   E. hardware   2.___

3. The entering of data into a computer system is the responsibility of the
   A. programmers   B. analysts
   C. data control clerk   D. data entry clerk
   E. computer operator   3.___

4. The MOST common input media is(are) the
   A. keypunch cards   B. magnetic tape
   C. magnetic disk   D. compact disk
   E. keyboard   4.___

5. The coding, testing, and debugging of computer software is the duty of the
   A. programmer   B. analyst
   C. operator   D. data control clerk
   E. data entry clerk   5.___

6. ____ is the term associated with the off-line preparation of data later submitted for processing with other data that has been prepared off-line.
   A. Timesharing   B. Batch processing
   C. Interactive processing   D. Real-time processing
   E. Aggregate processing   6.___

7. Multiple users share a single computer's resources in
   A. batch processing   B. interactive processing
   C. microprocessing   D. timesharing
   E. all of the above   7.___

8. The ____ field is the LARGEST consumer of computer products and services.
   A. science   B. business   C. health
   D. military   E. education   8.___

9. The ____ is considered to be an end-user of computer services.
   - A. accountant
   - B. programmer
   - C. operator
   - D. analyst
   - E. database administrator

9.____

10. In the organization of data, a group of related fields that pertains to a single data entity is called a
    - A. character
    - B. record
    - C. file
    - D. database
    - E. key field

10.____

11. A ____ field uniquely identifies a record in a file.
    - A. descriptive
    - B. indicative
    - C. normal key
    - D. key
    - E. none of the above

11.____

12. A collection of records within the SAME classification is called a
    - A. character
    - B. database
    - C. field
    - D. record
    - E. none of the above

12.____

13. The CORRECT hierarchy of data is
    - A. character, field, file, record
    - B. character, file, record, field
    - C. field, record, file, database
    - D. character, field, record, file, database
    - E. database, file, record, character, field

13.____

14. Which of the following data items located on a record would be BEST suited as a key field?
    - A. Hours worked
    - B. Rate of pay
    - C. Social security number
    - D. First name
    - E. Last name

14.____

15. An example of a logic function is determining that
    - A. 10 is 3 more than 7
    - B. 12 plus 6 is 18
    - C. 11 is an odd number
    - D. 10 is not equal to 20
    - E. all of the above

15.____

16. Which of the following is an example of a logic function performed by the computer?
    - A. Determining that 60 is an even number
    - B. Knowing that 120 is 12 dozen
    - C. Arranging a group of numbers in ascending sequence
    - D. Determining that 15 is 8 more than 7
    - E. Determining that 12 minus 7 is 5

16.____

17. Which of the following is an arithmetic process performed by the computer?
    - A. Arranging a group of numbers in descending order
    - B. Arranging a group of numbers in ascending order
    - C. Determining that 5 plus 4 is 9
    - D. Knowing that 6 is an even number
    - E. All of the above

17.____

18. An example of numeric data is   18.___
    A. 3
    B. THREE
    C. $300.45
    D. three hundred dollars forty-five cents
    E. none of the above

19. A coding technique used by banks to process checks is   19.___
    A. OCR   B. UPC   C. MICR
    D. Hollerith   E. SQL

20. The duplicate copy of an existing file is a(an)___file.   20.___
    A. duplicate   B. grandfather   C. backup
    D. archive   E. save

21. ____ code is used for the internal storage of data in   21.___
the computer.
    A. ASCII   B. EBCDIC   C. Binary
    D. Packed decimal   E. All of the above

22. An example of a peripheral device is the   22.___
    A. CPU   B. ALU   C. control unit
    D. disk drive   E. memory

23. The part of the computer that performs logical and   23.___
arithmetic functions is the
    A. memory   B. control unit   C. disk
    D. ALU   E. CPU

24. Of the following, the secondary storage media that offers   24.___
the FASTEST data storage and retrieval is the
    A. computer memory   B. magnetic tape
    C. magnetic disk   D. keypunch cards
    E. paper tape

25. An example of an input/output device is the   25.___
    A. magnetic tape   B. magnetic disk
    C. CPU   D. disk drive
    E. all of the above

_____

KEY (CORRECT ANSWERS)

1. E	11. D
2. E	12. E
3. D	13. D
4. C	14. C
5. A	15. D
6. B	16. C
7. D	17. C
8. B	18. A
9. A	19. C
10. B	20. C

21. E
22. D
23. D
24. C
25. D

TEST 2

DIRECTIONS: Each question or incomplete statement is followed by several suggested answers or completions. Select the one that BEST answers the question or completes the statement. *PRINT THE LETTER OF THE CORRECT ANSWER IN THE SPACE AT THE RIGHT.*

1. The computerized retrieval of microfilm is referred to as   1.___
   A. OCR   B. COM   C. microfax
   D. MICR   E. CAD/CAM

2. The ____ is a very high speed non-impact printer.   2.___
   A. daisy wheel   B. chain printer
   C. laser printer   D. plotter
   E. dot-matrix printer

3. A computer which inputs data from physical measurements   3.___
   such as heat, motion, or touch is called a ____ computer.
   A. digital   B. analog   C. mainframe
   D. micro   E. mini

4. A ____ computer performs general purpose, multiple con-   4.___
   current operations with many users.
   A. micro   B. mini   C. mainframe
   D. timesharing   E. All of the above

5. Some smaller computers are comparable to larger computers   5.___
   in performance, but are considered to be *task-oriented*.
   They may handle multiple users, but they primarily work
   on a single type of application such as accounting,
   billing, or inventory.
   This paragraph BEST describes ____ computers.
   A. mainframe   B. micro   C. mini
   D. super   E. general purpose

6. The MOST widely used computer language is   6.___
   A. Cobol   B. Pascal   C. RPG
   D. Fortran   E. Basic

7. The software which converts a high-level language like   7.___
   Fortran into the machine language which is directly under-
   stood by the computer is called a(n)
   A. preprocessor   B. multiplexor
   C. source originator   D. compiler
   E. all of the above

8. ____ is NOT a *high-level* computer language.   8.___
   A. Cobol   B. Basic   C. RPG
   D. PL/1   E. Assembler

9. ____ is used PRIMARILY in the scientific and engineering   9.____
   community.
   A. Cobol   B. Basic   C. Machine language
   D. PL/1   E. Fortran

10. An example of a computer language used effectively for   10.____
    business applications is
    A. Cobol   B. RPG   C. Basic
    D. PL/1   E. all of the above

11. Which of the following terms is CLOSELY associated with   11.____
    the term *structured programming*?
    A. HIPO   B. Top-down design
    C. Hierarchy chart   D. Modular programming
    E. All of the above

12. A storage capacity of 640K is APPROXIMATELY ____ bytes.   12.____
    A. 640,000,000   B. 64,000   C. 640,000
    D. 6,400,000   E. 640

13. A computer disk is divided into concentric circles called   13.____
    A. tracks   B. cylinders   C. rings
    D. sectors   E. segments

14. In order to ensure the accuracy of data stored on tape or   14.____
    disk, the computer will append a ____ to each byte of data.
    A. check digit   B. parity bit   C. check bit
    D. modula 11 bit   E. validation bit

15. Direct access is a feature of the   15.____
    A. magnetic tape   B. keypunch cards
    C. magnetic disk   D. compiler
    E. none of the above

16. Magnetic tape is BEST suited for situations where   16.____
    A. data is accessed sequentially
    B. VSAM is the data access method
    C. ISAM is the data access method
    D. data is accessed using direct access
    E. KSAM is the data access method

17. A term used to describe the algorithmic process of   17.____
    converting a key field into a storage location is
    A. hashing   B. ISAM   C. VSAM
    D. indexing   E. dynamic storage

18. The software which controls the general operating   18.____
    procedures of the computer is the
    A. applications program   B. source program
    C. object program   D. operating system
    E. systems program

19. The computer language used to DIRECTLY communicate with   19.____
    the computer's operating software is
    A. RPG   B. DOS   C. JCL
    D. VSAM   E. none of the above

20. A common pathway on which all data travels to and from   20.___
    the CPU to peripheral devices is the
        A. channel   B. line   C. bus
        D. modem   E. multiplexor

21. The ____ converts computer signals to be transferred   21.___
    over telephone lines and vice versa.
        A. coaxial cable   B. multiplexor
        C. modem   D. controller
        E. digital teleprocessor

22. *Baud* is a measurement of   22.___
        A. storage capacity   B. CPU performance
        C. disk speed   D. printer speed
        E. transmission speed

23. _____ is a type of network COMMONLY used on micro-   23.___
    computers.
        A. Narrowband   B. LAN   C. Star
        D. Ring   D. Hub

24. A type of computer that will handle the preliminary   24.___
    processing of data BEFORE it is sent to the mainframe
    computer is called a
        A. pre-processor   B. front-end processor
        C. back-end processor   D. minicomputer
        E. slave computer

25. The ____ would NOT be a member of the data processing   25.___
    staff in an organization.
        A. analyst   B. programmer   C. auditor
        D. operator   E. data entry clerk

KEY (CORRECT ANSWERS)

1. B		11. E	
2. C		12. C	
3. B		13. B	
4. C		14. B	
5. C		15. C	
6. A		16. A	
7. D		17. A	
8. E		18. D	
9. E		19. C	
10. E		20. C	

21. C
22. E
23. B
24. B
25. C

EXAMINATION SECTION

TEST 1

DIRECTIONS: Each question or incomplete statement is followed by several suggested answers or completions. Select the one that BEST answers the question or completes the statement. *PRINT THE LETTER OF THE CORRECT ANSWER IN THE SPACE AT THE RIGHT.*

1. The _____ on the data processing staff is responsible for determining if a new application should be developed.   1.___
   A. programmer   B. analyst
   C. operator   D. database administrator
   E. all of the above

2. A collection of files grouped together so that data may be independently retrieved from each file is a   2.___
   A. file   B. record
   C. database   D. file management system
   E. data bank

3. The data processing cycle consists of input,   3.___
   A. processing, output
   B. arithmetic, logic, output
   C. storage, output
   D. processing, storage, output
   E. arithmetic, logic, storage, output

4. Before any data may be processed, it MUST reside   4.___
   A. on tape   B. on keypunch cards
   C. in computer memory   D. on the video screen
   E. on the printer

5. _____ may be stored on magnetic disk.   5.___
   A. Characters   B. Fields   C. Records
   D. Databases   E. All of the above

6. An example of a source document is a   6.___
   A. bill produced by a computer
   B. keypunch card
   C. handwritten list of items to be entered into a computer
   D. checking statement sent by a bank to a customer
   E. all of the above

7. Data integrity refers to _____ entry of data into the computer system.   7.___
   A. accurate   B. reliable   C. timely
   D. all of the above E. none of the above

8. The process of arranging a list of names in alphabetical order is called   8.___
   A. indexing   B. sorting   C. reporting
   D. searching   E. selection

9. The MAIN components of a computerized report are 9.___
   A. heading, detail lines, summary
   B. data entry screen, editing area, data validation area
   C. heading, control breaks, summary
   D. heading, subtotal lines, summary
   E. heading and summary lines

10. ____ terminals are computer terminals which also have 10.___
    processing capabilities.
    A. Keyboard   B. Dumb
    C. Remote job entry   D. Intelligent
    E. Stand-alone

11. The process of transferring data over a communication line 11.___
    from a mainframe computer to a microcomputer is
    A. uploading   B. downloading
    C. modem transmission   D. electronic mail
    E. networking

12. During ____, data is entered onto storage media, then 12.___
    re-entered again to ensure the accuracy of the data.
    A. editing   B. validation checking
    C. bi-keying   D. key verification
    E. double verification

13. A(n) ____ printer is an example of a high-speed printer. 13.___
    A. ink jet   B. laser   C. dot matrix
    D. chain   E. all of the above

14. A(n) ____ report is NOT produced by a computer. 14.___
    A. detail   B. exception   C. projection
    D. summary   E. all of the above

15. A ____ video screen displays only one color. 15.___
    A. VGA   B. color   C. monochrome
    D. CRT   E. all of the above

16. The ____ printer is BEST suited to print graphic output. 16.___
    A. dot matrix   B. daisy wheel C. plotter
    D. chain   E. thermal

17. Which of the following can be used for entering data into 17.___
    a computer?
    A. OCR   B. Mouse   C. Keyboard
    D. Light pen   E. All of the above

18. Database management systems use a special class of 18.___
    commands in order that a user may facilitate extracting
    data from the database.
    This class of commands is called ____ language.
    A. query by example   B. query
    C. inquiry   D. programming
    E. procedure

19. An acceptable response time from when the user requests   19.___
    data from the computer to the time the user receives a
    response is under ____ seconds.
    A. 60   B. 30   C. 15   D. 10   E. 3

20. The part of computer memory which may be accessed by the   20.___
    user for storage and retrieving his own data is called
    A. RAM   B. ROM   C. EPROM   D. PROM   E. DROM

21. The part of the CPU which directs the sequence of   21.___
    instructions and flow of data is the
    A. ALU   B. control unit   C. memory
    D. logic unit   E. arithmetic unit

22. ____ is the placement on disk or tape of two or more con-   22.___
    secutive records in between interblock gaps.
    A. Gapping   B. Blocking   C. Staggering
    D. Sequencing   E. Sorting

23. When updating a sequential file,   23.___
    A. *only* the record being updated is changed
    B. *only* the record and those preceding it are changed
    C. the entire file must be read and rewritten
    D. *only* the record being updated and those following it
       are changed
    E. two new files are created

24. Sequential files are used PRIMARILY for   24.___
    A. backup data   B. on-line processing
    C. interactive processing   D. timesharing
    E. all of the above

25. In a hierarchial database, data is stored in a ____   25.___
    relationship.
    A. father-son   B. member-owner   C. sequential
    D. direct   E. none of the above

KEY (CORRECT ANSWERS)

1. B		11. B	
2. C		12. D	
3. D		13. E	
4. C		14. C	
5. E		15. C	
6. C		16. C	
7. D		17. E	
8. B		18. B	
9. A		19. E	
10. D		20. A	

21. B
22. B
23. C
24. A
25. B

TEST 2

DIRECTIONS: Each question or incomplete statement is followed by several suggested answers or completions. Select the one that BEST answers the question or completes the statement. *PRINT THE LETTER OF THE CORRECT ANSWER IN THE SPACE AT THE RIGHT.*

1. The ____ communication line allows the short distance (50-75 miles) transmission of data through the airwaves.
   A. satellite   B. fiber-optics   C. laser
   D. microwave   E. coaxial
              1.___

2. ____ data transmission permits *only* one character to be transmitted at a time.
   A. Full duplex   B. Half duplex   C. Asynchronous
   D. Parallel   E. Simplex
              2.___

3. During ____, the computer *asks* a terminal if it has data to process.
   A. polling   B. surveying   C. inquiry
   D. dialing   E. calling
              3.___

4. ____ is a centralized type of computer network used on larger computer systems.
   A. LAN   B. Star network
   C. Ring network   D. Distributed network
   E. All of the above
              4.___

5. An advantage of low-level languages over high-level languages is that low-level languages
   A. are easier to write in
   B. are easier to find and correct errors
   C. can make optimum use of computer resources
   D. need very few instructions to write a complete program
   E. all of the above are advantages
              5.___

6. The software to be loaded FIRST before any other software can be loaded into the computer is the
   A. applications program   B. utility programs
   C. operating system   D. compilers
   E. programming languages
              6.___

7. Which of the following is NOT an operating system?
   A. OS/VS   B. MS-DOS   C. UNIX
   D. OS2   E. Cobol
              7.___

8. A ____ graphically describes the flow of data through a system.
   A. data flow diagram   B. hierarchy chart
   C. pseudocode   D. HIPO chart
   E. Gantt chart
              8.___

9. A list of the files, records, fields, etc. used in a   9.___
system is maintained in a
   A. program maintenance notebook
   B. data dictionary
   C. system documentation manual
   D. operator's manual
   E. transaction log

10. A(n) ____ is generated by a computerized business system   10.___
to track accounting transactions back to their source .
   A. transaction log   B. data dictionary
   C. audit trail   D. system flowchart
   E. all of the above

11. A ____ is used to schedule the time it will take to   11.___
complete computer tasks or program development.
   A. system flowchart   B. data flow diagram
   C. Gantt chart   D. data dictionary
   E. transaction log

12. Which conversion method is used for converting a manual   12.___
system to a computerized system?
   A. Parallel   B. Direct
   C. Test-site   D. All of the above
   E. None of the above

13. The organization responsible for the standardization of   13.___
programming languages and procedures is
   A. NCAA   B. ANSI   C. NCAP   D. CODASYL   E. DLL

14. The process whereby a program is reviewed step by step   14.___
in an effort to uncover flaws in the program is called
   A. flowcharting   B. pseudocode
   C. structured walkthrough   D. IPO
   E. data flow diagramming

15. Which of the following is an application for personal   15.___
computers?
   A. Word processing
   B. Electronic spreadsheets
   C. Database management systems
   D. Computerized accounting systems
   E. All of the above

16. Which of the following is an entry-level position?   16.___
   A. Analyst   B. Applications programmer
   C. Systems programmer   D. Database administrator
   E. Lead programmer

17. *Computer security* refers to protection from   17.___
   A. unauthorized users
   B. abusive users
   C. misuse of computer resources
   D. disasters such as fire and flood
   E. all of the above

18. The process of transforming a telephone (analog) to a   18.____
    computer (digital) signal so that it may be understood
    by the computer system is called
        A. modulation   B. demodulation   C. analogation
        D. digitalization   E. multiplexing

19. The ____ computer numbering system uses both number and   19.___
    letter symbols to represent values.
        A. binary   B. digital   C. decimal
        D. octal   E. hexadecimal

20. One type of computer file contains data that is relatively   20.___
    static, that is, data that does not change on a regular
    basis. This file is treated as an authority on records
    which are associated with it.
    This paragraph BEST describes a(n) ____ file.
        A. transaction   B. index   C. master
        D. memory   E. authority

21. A ____ is a set of rules which governs the transmission   21.___
    of data over a communications channel.
        A. protocol   B. handshake   C. sequencer
        D. modem   E. algorithm

22. This technique is used to transmit large quantities of   22.___
    data from the CPU to tape or disk so that it can be output
    through a low-speed device such as a printer. The CPU is
    then free to process other data.
    This paragraph BEST describes the process of
        A. modulation   B. demodulation
        C. spooling   D. updating
        E. transaction processing

23. One type of computer memory uses disk or tape to store   23.___
    portions of software not in use. With this type of
    memory, the computer has almost unlimited main memory
    capacity.
    This paragraph BEST describes
        A. VLSI   B. VSAM
        C. virtual memory   D. partioned memory
        E. dynamic memory

24. *Throughput* measures computer   24.___
        A. memory capacity
        B. storage capacity
        C. speed at which work can be processed
        D. CPU speed
        E. all of the above

25. EBCDIC, ASCII, and Hollerith code are all   25.___
        A. hexadecimal codes
        B. binary codes
        C. zoned coding systems
        D. used on magnetic storage devices (disk and tape)
        E. used to represent numeric values only

KEY (CORRECT ANSWERS)

1.	D		11.	C
2.	C		12.	D
3.	A		13.	B
4.	B		14.	C
5.	C		15.	E
6.	C		16.	B
7.	E		17.	E
8.	A		18.	B
9.	B		19.	E
10.	C		20.	C

21. A
22. C
23. C
24. C
25. C

EXAMINATION SECTION
TEST 1

DIRECTIONS: Each question or incomplete statement is followed by several suggested answers or completions. Select the one that BEST answers the question or completes the statement. *PRINT THE LETTER OF THE CORRECT ANSWER IN THE SPACE AT THE RIGHT.*

1. Which of the following ASCII codes corresponds to the character *1*?
   A. 061　　　　B. 100　　　　C. 101　　　　D. 361

   1.___

2. Generally, the FIRST step in designing a data processing system is to
   A. draft a HIPO diagram
   B. select input/output and file descriptors
   C. draft a flowchart
   D. select the processing method

   2.___

3. A(n) _____ is the term for any signal or message that indicates the receipt of data or commands.
   A. indicator　　　　　　B. concession
   C. address　　　　　　　D. acknowledgement

   3.___

4. Which of the following aspects of data handling are MOST expensive?
   A. Validation and protection
   B. Storage and retrieval
   C. Collection and transcription
   D. Organization and aggregation

   4.___

5. The flowchart drawing shown at the right represents a _____ symbol.
   A. display
   B. document
   C. off-line storage
   D. connector

   5.___

6. What is the term for the reduction of a mass of data to a manageable form?
   A. Compression　　　　　B. File restructuring
   C. Summarizing　　　　　D. Aggregation

   6.___

7. In _____ processing, data is handled as soon as it is available.
   A. simultaneous　　　　B. batch
   C. distributed　　　　　D. transaction

   7.___

8. Which of the following is a linear data list in which elements are added and removed only from one end of the list?
   A. Stack　　　　B. String　　　　C. Queue　　　　D. B-tree

   8.___

9. When four binary digits are read as a single number, the
   _____ numbering system is being used.
   A. shorthand   B. quaternary
   C. decimal   D. hexadecimal

9.___

10. A company uses its data processing system to prepare a
    reminder notice for a customer whose payment deadline
    has passed.
    This is an example of
    A. summarization   B. control-break reporting
    C. issuance   D. selection

10.___

11. In an array with columns numbered from 4 through 13 and
    rows from 6 through 12, the MAXIMUM number of elements
    that can be stored is
    A. 56   B. 63   C. 70   D. 144

11.___

12. The symbol shown at the right represents
    a(n)
    A. *OR* gate
    B. inverter
    C. *NOR* gate
    D. *NAND* gate

12.___

13. When data is accessed from a database in response to an
    application program request, which of the following occurs
    FIRST?
    A. Data element is accessed and stored in a buffer of
       the database management system (DBMS).
    B. DBMS issues command to access data from secondary
       storage.
    C. Control unit transfers control to the DBMS.
    D. DBMS transfers data element to application program
       storage area.

13.___

14. An *interrupt* is
    A. a notation to the control unit that a condition has
       arisen that requires attention
    B. the arrest of data processing due to bit error
    C. the primary means by which a technician isolates
       computer failures
    D. an internal command which causes the computer to
       cease operation

14.___

15. In certain internal sort algorithms, the next logically
    sequential key in an unsorted list is chosen and placed
    in the next position in a growing sorted list.
    What is the term for this type of sort?
    A. Stable   B. Selection
    C. Sequential   D. Partition-exchange sort

15.___

16. A(n) _____ is NOT classified as a *simple* logical data structure. 16.___
    A. array   B. record   C. graph   D. string

17. Each of the following is a component of a control unit EXCEPT a 17.___
    A. compiler   B. register
    C. decoder   D. program counter

18. A data report shows information on the sales of a single product, with three subtotals and a grand total. 18.___
    This is an example of
    A. information retrieval   B. control-break reporting
    C. updating   D. summarizing

19. Which of the following rules applies to a computer's *AND* gate? 19.___
    The output is
    A. inactive only if all inputs are active
    B. active if any one of the inputs is active
    C. active only if all inputs are active
    D. inactive if any one of the inputs is active

20. A _____ is a data collision resolution technique in which a search for an empty location proceeds serially from the record's home address. 20.___
    A. collating sequence   B. double hashing
    C. multigraphing   D. linear probing

21. When a unit needs further information to define the required operation, that information is typically held in the 21.___
    A. register   B. control word
    C. instructions   D. memory

22. Each of the following is a typical application of stacks EXCEPT 22.___
    A. identifying windows in a screen management system
    B. inventory lists
    C. selecting the next packet to be processed from a communications line
    D. menu picks in a hierarchical menu system

23. Which of the following is represented by the flowchart symbol shown at the right? 23.___
    A. Connector symbol
    B. Manual action symbol
    C. Flow lines
    D. Communications-link symbol

24. The MAIN advantage associated with having a head node on   24.___
    a data list is
    A. conservation of space
    B. help in finding the end of a circular list
    C. improved performance when finding a node prior to any
       node on the list
    D. improved performance when deleting nodes from the
       list

25. In octal code, the binary number 101 111 011 would appear   25.___
    as
    A. 243   B. 7F   C. 573   D. DR

———

KEY (CORRECT ANSWERS)

1. A		11. C	
2. B		12. D	
3. D		13. C	
4. C		14. A	
5. A		15. B	
6. C		16. C	
7. D		17. A	
8. A		18. B	
9. D		19. C	
10. C		20. D	

21. B
22. C
23. D
24. B
25. C

———

TEST 2

DIRECTIONS: Each question or incomplete statement is followed by several suggested answers or completions. Select the one that BEST answers the question or completes the statement. *PRINT THE LETTER OF THE CORRECT ANSWER IN THE SPACE AT THE RIGHT.*

1. A customer withdraws $200 from her checking account at an automated teller machine, and that amount is immediately deducted from her account balance.
    This is an example of
    A. multi-key processing   B. control-break reporting
    C. real-time processing   D. data packing

    1.___

2. The quantity of characters in a data numbering system are denoted by the system's
    A. radix   B. code   C. array   D. digits

    2.___

3. Each of the following is an example of *linear* logical data structure EXCEPT
    A. linked list   B. queue
    C. general tree   D. stack

    3.___

4. Which basic computer element is represented by the symbol shown at the right?
    A. NOR gate
    B. Inverter
    C. Exclusive OR gate
    D. AND gate

    4.___

5. _____ is a technique for managing records on storage where a record's key value is mapped to an area of space that can hold multiple records.
    A. Cylinder addressing   B. Bucket addressing
    C. Multi-key processing   D. Sector addressing

    5.___

6. When a computer receives a halt instruction, each of the following is true EXCEPT the
    A. instruction-address counter holds the address of the next instruction to be executed
    B. results of the instruction executed prior to the halt instruction are left undisturbed by the halt instruction
    C. computer will not resume operation without manual intervention
    D. memory automatically stores the results of the instruction executed prior to the halt instruction

    6.___

7. When a binary operator appears between its operands, it
   is said to be using the _____ notation method of repre-
   senting an arithmetic expression.   7.___
   A. prefix   B. postfix
   C. insertion sort   D. infix

8. When data can be accessed without reference to previous   8.___
   data, the _____ access method is in effect.
   A. direct   B. sequential
   C. cross-keyed   D. indexed

9. The purpose of a HIPO diagram is to   9.___
   A. organize the instructions within a routine or sub-
      routine
   B. map out the physical components of a data processing
      system
   C. prioritize the instructions involved in storage and
      retrieval of data items
   D. list the steps involved in taking identified inputs
      and creating required files or outputs

10. A librarian keys in the title of a book on a display   10.___
    terminal to see whether it has been checked out.
    This is an example of
    A. sorting   B. information retrieval
    C. issuance   D. distributed processing

11. What is the term for unselective copying of memory   11.___
    contents to another storage medium?
    A. Dump   B. Rush   C. Scratch   D. Filigree

12. What is the term for the data structure that is a finite   12.___
    sequence of symbols taken from a character set?
    A. List   B. Queue   C. String   D. Stack

13. Which of the following types of numbering systems is a   13.___
    shorthand method for replacing a group of three binary
    digits with a single digit?
    A. Tertiary   B. Octal
    C. Hexadecimal   D. Triplex

14. When two unequal key values map to the same data address,   14.___
    _____ occurs.
    A. bubble sorting   B. concatenation
    C. a collision   D. inversion

15. A bank records all deposits made to customer accounts at   15.___
    the end of each work day.
    This is an example of
    A. batch processing   B. hashing
    C. distributed processing   D. control-break reporting

16. Each of the following is held in a computer's primary   16.___
    memory EXCEPT
    A. programs and data that have been passed to the
       computer for processing
    B. machine-language instructions
    C. output that is ready to be transmitted to an output
       device
    D. intermediate processing results

17. *Pushing* and *popping* data are terms used in reference to   17.___
    which data structure?
    A. Strings   B. Queues   C. B-trees   D. Stacks

18. Which of the following methods for file access makes use   18.___
    of fields which are used to identify each record in the
    file?
    A. Keyed   B. Distributed
    C. Sequential   D. Direct

19. Each of the following is an example of a *primitive* logical   19.___
    data structure EXCEPT
    A. character   B. list   C. boolean   D. integer

20. In hexadecimal code, the number 1110 1111 would appear as   20.___
    A. 6A   B. 116   C. EF   D. 192

21. Which of the following is a data collision resolution   21.___
    stragegy in which synonyms for a record are all stored
    in the file's primary address space?
    A. Separate-overflow addressing
    B. Linear probing
    C. Open addressing
    D. Double hashing

22. Typically, the jobs to be performed by a system, as well   22.___
    as the programs that will perform them, are controlled
    and selected by the
    A. subroutine   B. executive program
    C. compiler   D. directory

23. In a computer's *NOR* gate, the output is inactive   23.___
    A. *only* if all inputs are inactive
    B. if any one input is inactive
    C. *only* if all inputs are active
    D. if any one input is active

24. A company uses its data processing system to compose an   24.___
    employee phone book with names in alphabetical order.
    This is an example of
    A. sorting   B. b-tree hierarchy
    C. selection   D. issuance

25. Which of the following components of the arithmetic unit   25.___
    is capable of performing logical operations?
       A. Compiler   B. Carry-in   C. Counter   D. Adder

___

KEY (CORRECT ANSWERS)

1.	C		11.	A
2.	A		12.	C
3.	C		13.	B
4.	C		14.	C
5.	B		15.	A
6.	D		16.	B
7.	D		17.	D
8.	A		18.	A
9.	D		19.	B
10.	B		20.	C

21. C
22. B
23. D
24. A
25. D

___

EXAMINATION SECTION
TEST 1

DIRECTIONS: Each question or incomplete statement is followed by several suggested answers or completions. Select the one that BEST answers the question or completes the statement. *PRINT THE LETTER OF THE CORRECT ANSWER IN THE SPACE AT THE RIGHT.*

1. The structured approach aims to   1.___
   A. improve productivity
   B. reduce errors
   C. place more emphasis on design activities
   D. simplify programming logic
   E. all of the above

2. The creation of a hierarchy among components is called   2.___
   A. cohesion   B. coupling
   C. top-down   D. span of control
   E. all of the above

3. Subdividing tasks into subtasks is   3.___
   A. cohesion   B. levelling   C. splitting
   D. focusing   E. iteration

4. Each unit or task is known as a(n)   4.___
   A. module   B. sequence   C. selection
   D. coupling   E. span of control

5. A module   5.___
   A. is single purpose
   B. has a single entry point
   C. has a single exit point
   D. can control another module
   E. all of the above

6. A program is a collection of   6.___
   A. modules
   B. ideas
   C. cohesive iterative loops
   D. sentences or statements
   E. all of the above

7. Coupling is a measure of   7.___
   A. the number of statements in a module
   B. the number of modules in a program
   C. the interdependence of modules
   D. parent versus child modules
   E. number of IF statements in the program

8. Which of the following is NOT a type of module coupling?   8.___
   A. Stamp   B. External   C. Data
   D. Common   E. Control

9. Which type of module calls itself?   9.___
   A. Stamp   B. External   C. Data
   D. Context   E. Common

10. Which type of module receives more data than it can   10.___
    process?
    A. Data   B. Stamp   C. Content
    D. Common   E. External

11. The number of modules subservient to a parent module is   11.___
    called
    A. span of modules   B. recursive modules
    C. span of control   D. number of children
    E. none of the above

12. The ideal span of control is   12.___
    A. 5 to 9   B. 1 to 3
    C. 15 to 20   D. 1
    E. it doesn't matter

13. A graphic tool using diamonds, parallelograms, rectangles,   13.___
    ovals, and circles is
    A. data flow diagram   B. HIPO chart
    C. Nassi-Schniderman chart D. flowchart
    E. IPO chart

14. When drawing a flowchart, you should NOT   14.___
    A. cross lines
    B. draw from top to bottom
    C. draw from left to right
    D. use a template
    E. evenly space symbols

15. A system flowchart shows   15.___
    A. data conversion processes
    B. procedures to convert data
    C. detailed operations to perform on data
    D. module coupling
    E. span of control

16. A detail flowchart shows   16.___
    A. data conversion processes
    B. procedures to convert data
    C. detailed operations to perform on data
    D. module coupling
    E. span of control

17. Which of the following symbols is NOT used in a detail   17.___
    flowchart?
    A. Triangle   B. Oval   C. Parallelogram
    D. Rectangle   E. Diamond

18. Which of the following symbols is used to draw system   18.___
    flowcharts?
    A. Triangle   B. Oval   C. Parallelogram
    D. Rectangle   E. Diamond

19. Which of the following tools is CLOSELY associated with   19.___
the HIPO diagram?
    A. Data flow diagrams   B. Data dictionaries
    C. IPO   D. Detail flowchart
    E. Electronic spreadsheet

20. A synonym for a VTOC is a(n)   20.___
    A. IPO   B. structure chart
    C. HIPO   D. DFD
    E. Warnier-Orr diagram

21. A synonym for pseudocode is   21.___
    A. structured English   B. data dictionary
    C. data flow diagram   D. decision table
    E. decision tree

22. Which of the following is MOST similar to a decision table? 22.___
    A. Structured English   B. Data dictionary
    C. Data flow diagram   D. Condition table
    E. Decision tree

23. Which of the following can be used in place of a system   23.___
flowchart?
    A. IPO   B. VTOC
    C. Decision table   D. Decision flow network
    E. Detail flowchart

24. Which tool employs simple imperative sentences, omits   24.___
punctuation, and leaves out adjectives and adverbs?
    A. Detail flowchart   B. System flowchart
    C. Pseudocode   D. VTOC
    E. IPO

25. Which of the following is NOT a control structure?   25.___
    A. Sequence   B. Selection
    C. Iteration   D. Coupling
    E. All are control structures

KEY (CORRECT ANSWERS)

1. E		11. C	
2. C		12. A	
3. B		13. D	
4. A		14. A	
5. E		15. B	
6. A		16. C	
7. C		17. A	
8. B		18. A	
9. D		19. C	
10. B		20. B	

21. A
22. E
23. B
24. C
25. D

TEST 2

DIRECTIONS: Each question or incomplete statement is followed by several suggested answers or completions. Select the one that BEST answers the question or completes the statement. *PRINT THE LETTER OF THE CORRECT ANSWER IN THE SPACE AT THE RIGHT.*

1. Which control structure is sometimes called DO/WHILE?   1.___
   A. Sequence   B. Selection   C. Iteration
   D. Coupling   E. Cohesion

2. Which control structure shows events linearly?   2.___
   A. Sequence   B. Selection   C. Iteration
   D. Coupling   E. Data cohesion

3. Which control structure is also known as IF-THEN-ELSE?   3.___
   A. Sequence   B. Selection   C. Iteration
   D. Coupling   E. Span of control

4. Which of the following should NOT be followed when writing pseudocode?   4.___
   A. Indent subordinate sentences
   B. Use strong verbs
   C. Modules should be 24 or fewer statements
   D. IF-THEN do not have to have ELSE
   E. All of the above should be followed

5. The electronic spreadsheet was developed in the mid   5.___
   A. 1950's   B. 1960's   C. 1970's   D. 1980's   E. 1940's

6. The FIRST electronic spreadsheet is   6.___
   A. Multiplan   B. VisiCalc   C. 1-2-3
   D. SuperCalc   E. Symphony

7. Which symbol is NOT used when drawing a data flow diagram?   7.___
   A. Circle   B. Square
   C. Parallelogram   D. Arrow
   E. Three-sided rectangle

8. Which tool employs the +, =, [,]?   8.___
   A. Flowchart   B. Data dictionary
   C. Decision table   D. Decision tree
   E. Pseudocode

9. Which is NOT a rule to follow when writing a data dictionary definition?   9.___
   A. Words must be unique.
   B. Self-defining words need no further defining.
   C. Capitalize words.
   D. Use strong verbs.
   E. Avoid aliases.

10. The number of rules in a decision table with 4 conditions   10.___
    is
       A. 4   B. 8   C. 16   D. 32   E. 64

11. The action stub in a decision table occurs   11.___
       A. in the upper left
       B. in the upper right
       C. in the lower left
       D. in the lower right
       E. across the top of the table

12. The condition stub in a decision table occurs   12.___
       A. in the upper left
       B. in the upper right
       C. in the lower left
       D. in the lower right
       E. across the top of the table

13. The condition entry in a decision table occurs   13.___
       A. in the upper left
       B. in the upper right
       C. in the lower left
       D. in the lower right
       E. across the top of the table

14. The action entry in a decision table occurs   14.___
       A. in the upper left
       B. in the upper right
       C. in the lower left
       D. in the lower right
       E. across the top of the table

15. The title, author, and date written in a decision table   15.___
    occur
       A. in the upper left
       B. in the upper right
       C. in the lower left
       D. in the lower right
       E. across the top of the table

16. Which tool is read left to right and top down?   16.___
       A. System flowchart   B. Detail flowchart
       C. Data flow diagram   D. Warnier-Orr diagram
       E. Nassi-Schneiderman chart

17. Which tool uses the { to group items?   17.___
       A. System flowchart   B. Detail flowchart
       C. Data flow diagram   D. Warnier-Orr chart
       E. Nassi-Schneiderman chart

18. Which tool uses rectangles divided into halves?   18.___
       A. System flowchart   B. Detail flowchart
       C. Data flow diagram   D. Warnier-Orr diagram
       E. Nassi-Schneiderman chart

19. Which of the following is NOT the **purpose** of a walk-   19.___
through?
    A. Uncover errors
    B. Serve as a project management tool
    C. Serve as a teaching device
    D. Serve to motivate others to produce better work
    E. Serve as an evaluation device

20. Where are walkthroughs appropriate?   20.___
    A. After receipt of a user request
    B. After management has made a decision
    C. During development
    D. During review and assignment of tasks
    E. Walkthroughs are appropriate at any time

KEY (CORRECT ANSWERS)

1.	A	11.	C
2.	B	12.	A
3.	B	13.	B
4.	E	14.	D
5.	C	15.	E
6.	B	16.	D
7.	C	17.	D
8.	B	18.	E
9.	D	19.	E
10.	C	20.	C

EXAMINATION SECTION

TEST 1

1. A series of jobs that are executed one at a time, according to set procedures indicating the sequence in which they are to be executed is BEST described as
   - A. job stream
   - B. run schedule
   - C. operation schedule
   - D. run time sequence
   - E. execution sequence

   1.___

2. Which is NOT an advantage of a VS (Virtual Storage) system?
   - A. More jobs can run concurrently.
   - B. Pages of data or instructions required by a. program need not be stored contiguously in memory.
   - C. Real memory is better utilized.
   - D. More throughput is generally achieved.
   - E. An entire program is loaded in memory when it is. executed

   2.___

3. Which of the following would be an example of JCL statement?
   - A. ＼Off
   - B. New Payroll
   - C. A＞Compile
   - D. //Job MARO02
   - E. Data EOF, -999

   3.___

4. Record counts, batch totals, post-run totals, document counts, etc. are the responsibility of
   - A. systems analysis and design section
   - B. data control section
   - C. operations manager
   - D. DCOM
   - E. programmers

   4.___

5. The _____ should contain the instructions and JCL to initiate a job.
   - A. system flowchart
   - B. run manual
   - C. operator's guide
   - D. computer program
   - E. applications manual

   5.___

6. The procedures of labeling tapes and disks, reviewing error statistics, pulling tapes and disks for use, and maintaining documentation is the responsibility of the
   - A. data control section
   - B. librarian
   - C. programmers
   - D. computer operator
   - E. DCOM

   6.___

7. The _____ provides instructions for recovering a canceled job.
   - A. recall procedure manual
   - B. job control manual
   - C. restart procedure manual
   - D. run manual
   - E. standards manual

   7.___

8. The installation and tailoring of an operating system   8.___
   towards the needs of an organization is performed during
   the ____ procedure.
   A. bootup   B. SYSGEN   C. startup
   D. abend   E. all of the above

9. The ____ is generated by the operating system when an   9.___
   application program is suspended.
   A. abend   B. interrupt   C. crash
   D. system halt   E. check digit

10. When a system is IPLed, the computer
    A. is restarted and the operating system is loaded   10.___
    B. system has halted due to an error condition
    C. system has halted due to instructions issued by
       the operator
    D. system is being reconfigured to support different
       I/O devices
    E. none of the above

11. ____ is a type of interrupt whereby the application makes a 11.___
    request to the operating system.
    A. External   B. Machine check   C. I/O
    D. Program   E. Supervisor call

12. ____ is a type of interrupt whereby an improper program   12.___
    condition (such as an illegal arithmetic operation) is
    detected by the hardware.
    A. External   B. Machine check   C. I/O
    D. Program   E. Supervisor call

13. ____ is a type of interrupt whereby a signal is sent to   13.___
    the control unit indicating that data has been read or
    written.
    A. External   B. Machine check   C. I/O
    D. Program   E. Supervisor call

14. The ____ stores the operation code of the instruction   14.___
    currently being executed and the memory address of the
    next instruction to be executed.
    A. mask   B. PSW   C. JCL
    D. op code   E. supervisor call

15. The ____ library contains the programs that make up   15.___
    the operating system.
    A. procedure   B. private   C. system
    D. relocatable   E. source statement

16. The ____ library is used to catalog frequently used sets   16.___
    of control statements and linkage editor statements.
    A. procedure   B. private   C. system
    D. relocatable   E. source statement

17. The ____ is used to separate continuous form reports.   17.___
    A. separator   B. decollator   C. burster
    D. printer   E. report disengagor

18. Magnetic tape features ____ access.   18.___
    A. random   B. direct   C. sequential
    D. VSAM   E. ISAM

19. Magnetic disk features ____ access.   19.___
    A. random   B. direct   C. sequential
    D. indexed   E. all of the above

20. Which type of storage media is best suited to provide   20.___
    for the backup of transaction and master files, off-line
    storage, and communication between two different computer
    systems?
    A. Magnetic disk   B. Floppy disk
    C. Magnetic tape   D. Keypunch cards
    E. All of the above

21. On magnetic tape, ____ separates the physical records   21.___
    from the tape label information.
    A. leader   B. tape label
    C. load point marker   D. end point marker
    E. tape mark

22. Most mainframes (IBM, for example) use ____ code for   22.___
    recording data on magnetic tape.
    A. ASCII   B. EBCDIC   C. BCD
    D. binary   E. DIC

23. When using a disk drive, the ____ indicator is turned   23.___
    on if an unsafe condition exists on the device.
    A. DISABLE   B. INVALID DLBL
    C. INVALID LOGICAL UNIT   D. SELECT LOCK
    E. WRONG PACK

24. ____ occurs during a hardware or software failure.   24.___
    A. SYSINT   B. Head crash   C. Abend
    D. SYSGEN   E. All of the above

25. Input data accumulated and processed in large groups   25.___
    as opposed to a continuous stream is called ____.
    processing.
    A. on-line   B. real time   C. batch
    D. off-line   E. sequential

KEY (CORRECT ANSWERS)

1. A	6. B	11. E	16. A	21. E
2. E	7. C	12. D	17. C	22. B
3. D	8. B	13. C	18. C	23. D
4. B	9. B	14. B	19. E	24. C
5. B	10. A	15. C	20. C	25. C

TEST 2

Each question or incomplete statement is followed by several suggested answers or completions. Select the one that *BEST* answers the question or completes the statement. *PRINT THE LETTER OF THE CORRECT ANSWER IN THE SPACE AT THE RIGHT.*

1. Operating systems software perform ____ management.   1.____
   A. data   B. resource   C. job
   D. all of the above   E. none of the above

2. A(n) ____ is a location within computer memory or auxiliary   2.____
   memory (tapes, disks, etc.).
   A. byte   B. binary digit   C. address
   D. K (kilobyte) E. variable

3. A ____ is a temporary storage area where data waiting to be   3.____
   input or output is stored.
   A. channel   B. bus
   D. buffer   E. multiplexor   C. UNIBUS

4. A ____ is a point in a program when it can be restarted if it 4.____
   was canceled.
   A. load point marker   B. PSW
   C. checkpoint restart   D. restart point
   E. resumation point

5. A program that translates a source program in a high level   5.____
   computer language (such as COBOL or FORTRAN) into the
   machine language version of the program, the object module,
   is called a(n)
   A. interpreter   B. compiler   C. linker
   D. library   E. translator

6. Hexadecimal is a base ____ numbering system.   6.____
   A. 2   B. 8   C. 10   D. 12   E. 16

7. Evaluating methods and procedures of processing data and   7.____
   instituting procedures to prevent misuse of hardware and/or
   software is the responsibility of the ____. This person
   is usually an expert in accounting and data processing
   procedures.
   A. EDP auditor
   B. computer operator
   C. data control clerk
   D. data processing operations manager
   E. CIS manager

8. When a file protection ring is mounted onto a tape, data   8.____
   may
   A. be both read from and written to the tape
   B. be read from the tape only
   C. be written from the tape only
   D. not be read or written from the tape
   E. none of the above

9. The ____ does many of the pre-processing routines   9.___
   associated with telecommunications. For example, it
   may process a great many individual transactions before
   sending them on to final processing by the mainframe
   computer.
   A. minicomputer   B. back end processor
   C. front end processor   D. dedicated processor
   E. modem

10. ____ is a type of system where only the necessary soft-   10.___
   ware is in memory as a job is run. Other software resides
   on auxiliary storage and is called into memory as it is
   needed. Using this technique, computer memory is virtually
   unlimited.
   A. VS (Virtual Storage)   B. Dynamic memory
   C. Core memory   D. Sequential storage
   E. Extensible memory

11. When a computer is responding to commands issued by an   11.___
   applications program, it is said to be working in a(n)
   A. applications mode   B. object mode
   C. supervisory state   D. wait state
   E. problem state

12. ____ is NOT normally the responsibility of the console   12.___
   operator.
   A. Monitoring the execution of both batch and on-line
      jobs
   B. Transmitting messages to users
   C. Initiating job streams
   D. Performing SYSGENs
   E. Performing restart procedures

13. When a program is interrupted during execution time, the 13.___
   operator should ____ to determine the cause of the error.
   A. IPL the system
   B. correct the errors in the application program that
      caused the interrupt
   C. recheck the job run sheet to ensure all directions
      were followed
   D. call system engineers
   E. proceed to the next PSW

14. ____ is used to indicate exactly what was stored in memory 14.___
   at the time of an unrecoverable program error.
   A. PSW   B. Abend report
   C. Source listing   D. Memory dump
   E. Checkpoint restart

15. The ____ error checking routine determines if the correct 15.___
   number of bits has been transmitted to or from the CPU
   during input/output operations.
   A. checkpoint   B. validity bit
   C. parity check   D. machine check
   E. none of the above

16. Of the following input devices, ____ is being used less   16. ___
    frequently by data operations centers
    A. OCR   B. magnetic tape units
    C. magnetic disk units   D. card readers
    E. optical disk units

17. Which of the following statement is NOT true concerning   17. ___
    impact printers. They
    A. can provide letter quality output
    B. may use different fonts
    C. may use continuous forms
    D. may not print multi-part forms
    E. may print graphic output

18. The fastest type of printer is the ____ printer.   18. ___
    A. dot matrix   B. daisy wheel
    C. thermal   D. line
    E. laser

19. A JCL statement to assign a printer may be   19. ___
    A. *EOF DBLB   B. //ASSGN SYSOO6, SYSLST
    C. //ASSGN PRI   D. * $$ LST
    E. * $$ LST FNO=SYSOO6

20. The ____ is used on a printer to help control the verti-   20. ___
    cal alignment of forms in the printer.
    A. control buffer or carriage control tape
    B. reset key
    C. carriage key
    D. computer program
    E. tractor feed

21. The tape label contains   21. ___
    A. the volume number of the reel of tape
    B. the expiration date of the file
    C. label information
    D. all of the above

22. If a nine-track tape has a blocking factor of 12, how   22. ___
    many logical records are read into memory at a time?
    A. 1   B. 9   C. 12   D. 25   E. none of the above

23. When using magnetic data and a data check error occurs,   23. ___
    the FIRST action taken by the operator should be to
    A. remove the tape
    B. restore the tape from a back up tape
    C. change the density of the tape
    D. issue a command to read (or write) the tape a
       certain amount of times
    E. no operator action should be taken, it is the
       responsibility of the operating system to handle
       the matter.

24. Which is NOT a responsibility of the operator in
respect to magnetic tape?
   A. Determining the blocking factor of tapes
   B. Maintaining the backups
   C. Setting up JCL statements to use the tapes
   D. Making sure tapes are returned to correct storage
   areas
   E. Maintaining the tape log

24.___

25. A type of file organization used with disks that
utilizes a unique key to identify the storage address
of a record is the
   A. sequential
   B. dynamic
   C. indexed sequential access method
   D. volatile
   E. database

25.___

_____

KEY (CORRECT ANSWERS)

1.	D	11.	E
2.	C	12.	D
3.	D	13.	C
4.	C	14.	D
5.	B	15.	C
6.	E	16.	D
7.	A	17.	D
8.	B	18.	E.
9.	C	19.	B
10.	A	20.	A

21.	E
22.	C
23.	D
24.	A
25.	C

_____

EXAMINATION SECTION
TEST 1

DIRECTIONS: Each question or incomplete statement is followed by several suggested answers or completions. Select the one that BEST answers the question or completes the statement. *PRINT THE LETTER OF THE CORRECT ANSWER IN THE SPACE AT THE RIGHT.*

1. A database uses _____ to identify information.   1.___
   A. record numbers   B. register addresses
   C. field names   D. directories

2. _____ could be added to a database in order to increase   2.___
   the number of search and access points available to a
   user.
   A. Subject discriptors   B. Partitions
   C. Term authority lists   D. Call programs

3. The central idea behind the management of a database is   3.___
   A. procedural and nonprocedural interfaces
   B. minimal redundancy and minimal storage space
   C. physical data independence
   D. the separation of data description and data manipula-
   tion

4. Which of the following is NOT a type of query language   4.___
   operator used in database searches?
   A. Object-oriented   B. Logical
   C. Relational   D. Mathematical

5. When accessing a record in an indexed file, which of the   5.___
   following steps would be performed FIRST?
   A. Accessing the index
   B. Disk access to the record or bucket
   C. Data transfer from disk to main program memory
   D. Relative address conversion to absolute address

6. A database management system (DBMS) that employs a   6.___
   hierarchy, but may relate each lower-level data element
   to more than one parent element, is classified specifically as a(n) _____ DBMS.
   A. object-oriented   B. network
   C. relational   D. aggregational

7. A value-added field might be added to a database in order   7.___
   to
   A. standardize field formats
   B. estimate the disk capacity for a full database
   C. provide indexing consistency
   D. improve retrieval

8. Each of the following disks is a type of direct-access   8.___
   disk-storage system EXCEPT
      A. moving-head   B. floppy
      C. moving-capstan   D. fixed-head

9. In determining an appropriate file organization, three   9.___
   principal factors must be considered.
   Which of the following is NOT one of these factors?
      A. Volatility   B. Conversion
      C. Activity   D. Size

10. A _____ file is used to update or modify data in a   10.___
    master file.
       A. descriptor   B. transaction
       C. secondary   D. conversion

11. Which of the following steps in designing and using a   11.___
    database would be performed FIRST?
       A. Selecting a name for the file
       B. Deciding the form into which information should be
          stored
       C. Data definition
       D. Defining the type of data to be stored in each field

12. Each of the following is an advantage associated with the 12.___
    use of a DBMS over a flat-file system EXCEPT
       A. fewer storage requirements
       B. better data integrity
       C. lower software costs
       D. lower operating costs

13. Memory storage space that is not directly addressable by   13.___
    processor instructions, but by specialized I/O instruc-
    tions, is called
       A. allocated memory   B. secondary storage
       C. internal storage   D. main memory

14. Which of the following is NOT a disadvantage associated   14.___
    with sequential file processing?
       A. Master files must be sorted into key field sequence.
       B. Files are only current immediately after an update.
       C. Files are difficult to design.
       D. Transaction files must be stored in the same key.

15. When data is updated in some, but not all, of the files   15.___
    in which it appears, _____ has occurred.
       A. data confusion   B. data dependence
       C. cross-keying   D. data redundancy

16. The MOST common medium for direct-access storage is   16.___
       A. optical disk   B. magnetic tape
       C. hard card   D. magnetic disk

17. The purpose of *hashing* is to
    A. discover an unpartitioned sector onto which data may be written
    B. determine a schedule by which batch-processed data may be submitted to the computer
    C. create a buffer delay between data entry and output during interactive processing
    D. convert the key field value for a record to the address of the record on a file

17.___

18. What is the term for the description of a specific set of data corresponding to a model of an enterprise, which is obtained by using a particular data description language?
    A. Schema   B. Descriptor
    C. Object instance   D. Conceptualization

18.___

19. In a sequential file, records are arranged in sequence according to one or more
    A. query languages   B. column numbers
    C. key fields   D. hash marks

19.___

20. Which of the following is NOT a mathematical query language operator used in database searches?
    A. +   B. >=   C. ^   D. /

20.___

21. In _____ file organization, the cost per each transaction processed remains about the same as the percent of records accessed on a file increases.
    A. sequential   B. hashed
    C. indexed sequential   D. random

21.___

22. For more complex data types, such as those used in multimedia applications, what type of DBMS would be MOST useful?
    A. Hierarchical   B. Relational
    C. Object-oriented   D. Network

22.___

23. When determining how many generations of a file to retain in a database, the PRIMARY factor is usually
    A. hardware capabilities
    B. storage space
    C. whether files are keyed or indexed
    D. probability of need to access old data for recovery purposes

23.___

24. When data is transferred from a user program to secondary storage, it first passes through
    A. program private memory   B. file system buffers
    C. I/O buffers   D. program code

24.___

25. In order to maintain files in a database, each of the following operations is typically required EXCEPT
    A. balancing index trees

25.___

B. altering the file system's directory
C. changing field widths
D. adding fields to records

KEY (CORRECT ANSWERS)

1. C		11. B	
2. A		12. C	
3. D		13. B	
4. A		14. C	
5. A		15. A	
6. B		16. D	
7. D		17. D	
8. C		18. A	
9. B		19. C	
10. B		20. B	

21. D
22. C
23. D
24. D
25. B

TEST 2

Each question or incomplete statement is followed by several suggested answers or completions. Select the one that BEST answers the question or completes the statement. *PRINT THE LETTER OF THE CORRECT ANSWER IN THE SPACE AT THE RIGHT.*

1. An installation has two tape drives and one disk drive. An application program requires access to three sequential files: an old master file, a transaction file, and an updated master file.
   Typically, the _____ file should be stored on the disk.
   A. old master
   B. transaction
   C. updated master
   D. both versions of the master

   1.___

2. The purpose of *record blocking* is to
   A. allow multiple records to be brought into main memory in a single access to secondary storage
   B. create the illusion of a *virtual device* for the program until the spooler copies a record to the real device
   C. allocate more free buffer space to a file prior to run-unit determination
   D. offload responsibilities for building data paths from the CPU

   2.___

3. Entries in a database's secondary key tables (index files), which tell the computer where a data is stored on the disk, are
   A. logical records
   B. data addresses
   C. physical records
   D. secondary keys

   3.___

4. Of the types of file organization below, which involves the LOWEST volatility?
   A. Direct
   B. Sequential
   C. Master-keyed
   D. Indexed

   4.___

5. Typically each of the following elements is defined during the *data definition* process EXCEPT
   A. field types
   B. field names
   C. number of columns
   D. width of fields

   5.___

6. A database's master index contains
   A. the key values for an indexed sequential file
   B. the machine code for every field in a given set of records
   C. the logical record for every randomly-accessed file
   D. each field's physical location on a disk pack

   6.___

7. Which of the following types of information would MOST likely be stored in a logic field?   7.___
   A. Calendar month/day/year
   B. A patient or customer's mailing address
   C. Numbers that may later be involved in some mathematical calculations
   D. The designation of an employee's status is hourly or salaried

8. When determining how frequently a sequential master file should be updated, each of the following factors should be considered EXCEPT   8.___
   A. activity ratio
   C. storage space
   B. rate of data change
   D. urgency for current data

9. Which of the following programs is a file manager, rather than a DBMS?   9.___
   A. Q&A   B. FoxPro   C. Approach   D. Paradox

10. Which of the following is NOT an advantage associated with the use of indexed file processing?   10.___
    A. No need for hashing algorithm
    B. Random access is faster than direct processing
    C. Can function with applications required for both sequential and direct processing
    D. Access to specific records faster than sequential processing

11. Of the query language operators listed below, which is mathematical?   11.___
    A. .AND.   B. SUB   C. <   D. SQRT(N)

12. A collection of records may sometimes be structured as a file on secondary storage, rather than as a data structure in main memory.   12.___
    Which of the following is NOT a possible reason for this?
    A. Permanence of storage
    B. Security concerns
    C. Size of collection
    D. Selective access requirements

13. What is the term for the disk rotation time needed for the physical record to pass under read/write heads?   13.___
    A. Transaction time
    C. Head displacement time
    B. Latency time
    D. Transfer time

14. The subset of a database schema required by a particular application program is referred to as a(n)   14.___
    A. root
    C. logical structure
    B. user's view
    D. node

15. Which of the following steps in designing and using a   15.___
    database would be performed LAST?
       A. Defining the type of data that will be stored in
          each field
       B. Assigning field names
       C. Data definition
       D. Defining the width of alphanumeric and numeric fields

16. What type of database structure organizes data in the form   16.___
    of two-dimensional tables?
       A. Relational   B. Network
       C. Logical   D. Hierarchical

17. What is the term for the specific modules that are   17.___
    capable of reading and writing buffer contents on devices?
       A. Spoolers   B. Device handlers
       C. I/O managers   D. Memory allocators

18. Each of the following is a disadvantage associated with   18.___
    the use of a DBMS EXCEPT
       A. extensive conversion costs
       B. possible wide distribution of data losses and damage
       C. reduced data security
       D. start-up costs

19. _____ decisions about a database begin after a feasibility   19.___
    study and continue to be refined throughout the design
    and creation process.
       A. Procedural   B. Structural
       C. Conversion   D. Content

20. Each of the following is an advantage associated with   20.___
    direct file processing EXCEPT
       A. ability to update several files at the same time
       B. no need for separate transaction files
       C. files do not have to be sorted into key field
          sequence
       D. fewer storage space required than for sequential
          processing

21. The core of any file management system accesses   21.___
    secondary storage through
       A. the I/O manager   B. file system buffers
       C. relative addressing   D. key access

22. Each of the following is a responsibility typically   22.___
    belonging to a file system EXCEPT
       A. maintaining directories
       B. interfacing the CPU with a secondary storage device
       C. establishing paths for data flow between main memory
          and secondary storage
       D. buffering data for delivery to the CPU or secondary
          devices

23. In a hierarchical database, there are several phone   23.___
    numbers belonging to a single address.
    This is an example of
       A. vector data aggregate   B. data dependence
       C. data confusion   D. data redundancy

24. A DBMS might access the data dictionary for each of the   24.___
    following purposes EXCEPT
       A. change the description of a data field
       B. to determine if a data element already exists before
          adding
       C. request and deliver information from the database to
          the user
       D. determine what application programs can access what
          data elements

25. _____ would MOST likely be stored in a memo field.   25.___
       A. A revisable listing of symptoms specific to a
          particular ailment
       B. The designation of a patient's gender (male/female)
       C. A patient's billing number
       D. The date of a patient's last visit

———

KEY (CORRECT ANSWERS)

1. B		11. D	
2. A		12. B	
3. A		13. B	
4. B		14. B	
5. C		15. D	
6. A		16. A	
7. D		17. B	
8. C		18. C	
9. A		19. B	
10. B		20. D	

21. A
22. B
23. A
24. C
25. A

———

EXAMINATION SECTION

TEST 1

DIRECTIONS: Each question or incomplete statement is followed by several suggested answers or completions. Select the one that *BEST* answers the question or completes the statement. *PRINT THE LETTER OF THE CORRECT ANSWER IN THE SPACE AT THE RIGHT.*

1. Data Processing is the 1.____
   A. input and output of data
   B. transformation of data into information
   C. production of computer generated reports
   D. collection and dissemination of data
   E. none of the above

2. The CORRECT hierarchy of data is 2.____
   A. field, file, record, database
   B. character, field, record, file, database
   C. record, file, field, database
   D. bit, byte, record, database
   E. character, file, record, field, database

3. Which of the following is an update operation? 3.____
   A. Adding data
   B. Deleting data
   C. Changing data
   D. All of the above
   E. None of the avove

4. The ____ are three MAIN components of a computer generated 4.____
report.
   A. Control breaks, summaries and headings
   B. Detail lines, control breaks and graphs
   C. Headings, detail lines and summary lines
   D. Page breaks, headings and control breaks
   E. Columns, rows and totals

5. A computer generated report with control breaks must have 5.____
   A. the data organized in random order
   B. the data being produced from at least two files
   C. the data sorted on a control field
   D. page breaks on each control field
   E. at least two control breaks to be meaningful

6. The *primary* types of data processing environments in 6.____
existence today are
   A. batch and real-time
   B. real-time and on-line
   C. transaction and batch
   D. batch and on-line
   E. on-line and real-time

7. The FIRST step in solving a problem with a computer   7.___
   is
   A. coding
   B. debugging
   C. problem analysis
   D. system analysis
   E. problem definition with tools such as flowcharts or
      data flow diagrams

8. In the hierarchy of arithmetic operations, the operation   8.___
   with the HIGHEST priority is
   A. addition   B. multiplication
   C. exponentiation   D. parenthesis
   E. division

9. If A = 10, B = 20 and C = 30, what would be the result of   9.___
   the following operation?
   A * B + C * A
   A. 2,300   B. 500
   C. 400   D. 3,000
   E. none of these

10. If A = 5, B = 10 and C = 15, what would be the result of   10.___
    the following operation?
    A + C / (C + A)
    A. 1   B. 5.75   C. 10.5   D. 20   E. 15

11. A(n) ____ is a formula developed to solve a problem.   11.___
    A. computer program   B. algorithm
    C. flowchart   D. problem definition
    E. all of the above

12. The two MAIN data types are   12.___
    A. numeric and non-numeric
    B. alphabetic and alphanumeric
    C. numeric and alphabetic
    D. arithmetic and logical
    E. alphabetic and special characters

Questions 13 - 19

DIRECTION: Use the following flowchart symbols to answer
            questions 13 - 19

13. Which is used for commenting flowcharts?   13.___

14. Which is a process symbol?   14.___

15. Which is a decision box?   15.___

16. Which is a terminal?   16.___

17. Which is an input output symbol?   17.___

18. Which symbol would be BEST suited for the following   18.___
    expression? Is A > B?

19. Which symbol would be BEST suited for the following   19.___
    expression? Let tax = sale-price * .08?

20. An advantage of using a flowchart is that   20.___
    A. it is easy to update
    B. it is well suited for long problems
    C. its symbols are very easily memorized
    D. it graphically represents a problem
    E. all of the above are advantages

21. Flowcharting does NOT indicate   21.___
    A. flow lines   B. sequence
    C. line numbers   D. repetition or looping
    E. logical operations

22. A ____ keeps and maintains the content and description of 22.___
    variable names, file, and field names.
    A. database   B. data dictionary
    C. encyclopedia of data   D. data descriptor
    E. computer program

23. The ____ is the part of a program which may be repeated   23.___
    A. loop   B. data structure
    C. repetition structure   D. logic structure
    E. subroutine structure

24. Employee gross-pay is calculated by multiplying hours by 24.___
    rate. A tax rate of 8% is deducted before arriving at
    net -pay.
    Which equation would describe the calculation of gross-pay?
    A. Gross-pay = hours * rate * tax-rate
    B. Gross-pay = hours * rate - tax-rate
    C. Gross-pay = (hours * rate) - .08
    D. Gross-pay = 8 - (hours * rate)
    E. None of these

25. If you deposit $1,000 in a savings account at 8% interest 25.___
    for one year, at the end of the year there will be $1,080.
    Which equation would determine the amount in the bank? Amount = 1000
    A. 8   B. .08   C. 108   D. 1.08   E. 8%

KEY (CORRECT ANSWERS)

1.	B	11.	B
2.	B	12.	A
3.	D	13.	D
4.	C	14.	A
5.	C	15.	C
6.	D	16.	B
7.	C	17.	E
8.	D	18.	C
9.	B	19.	A
10.	B	20.	D

21. C
22. B
23. A
24. C
25. D

___

TEST 2

DIRECTIONS: Each question or incomplete statement is followed
by several suggested answers or completions. Select
the one that *BEST* answers the question or completes
the statement. *PRINT THE LETTER OF THE CORRECT
ANSWER IN THE SPACE AT THE RIGHT.*

1. The three *primary* program logic structures are   1.___
    A. looping, branching and sequence
    B. sequence, selection and iteration
    C. arithmetic, logic and sequence
    D. looping, sequence and logic
    E. arithmetic, logic and branching

2. Two basic symbols used by hierarchy charts are   2.___
    A. flow lines and circles
    B. process blocks (rectangles) and squares
    C. decision boxes and flow lines
    D. parallelograms and flow lines
    E. flow lines and process blocks (rectangles)

3. A ____ is a violation of the rules made by the programmer.   3.___
    A. logic error   B. structure error
    C. syntax error   D. bug
    E. slip

4. ____ verifies transaction data at all input, processing,   4.___
    and output points.
    A. Verification   B. An audit trail
    C. A transaction log   D. A transaction journal
    E. A ledger

5. ____ file organization arranges files in input sequence.   5.___
    A. Random   B. Direct
    C. Sequential   D. Relative
    E. Indexed

6. ____ refers to the process of examining a program design   6.___
    and reviewing the logic of a program with test data.
    A. Debugging   B. Desk checking
    C. Stepwise refinement   D. Verification
    E. Logic testing

7. This type of file organization allows a single record to be 7.___
    accessed without accessing the entire file. The location
    of the record to be accessed is relative to the position
    of the first record in the file.
    This paragraph refers to ____ access.
    A. direct   B. random
    C. serial   D. relative
    E. indexed

8. A ____ is a variable which will keep track of the number   8.____
   of occurrences of a certain transaction.
   A. counter   B. accumulator   C. totaler
   D. tally   E. register

9. The ____ report will list all or most of the information   9.____
   in a file.
   A. summary   B. detail   C. transaction
   D. exception   E. monitor

10. Data is *originally* recorded in the ____ document.   10.____
    A. transaction   B. object   C. original
    D. source   E. master

11. This verification technique confirms that data being   11.____
    input meets certain input criteria. The data being
    entered may be compared to a list of values.
    This paragraph refers to the
    A. range test   B. matching values
    C. control totals   D. required field
    E. class test

12. This verification technique confirms that data falls   12.____
    within certain limit of values.
    This statement refers to the
    A. range test   B. matching values
    C. control totals   D. required field
    E. class test

13. The binary (base 2) symbol equivalent to the decimal   13.____
    (base 10) number 31 is
    A. 31   B. 1111   C. 11111   D. 1011   E. none of these

14. The binary (base 2) symbol equivalent to the decimal   14.____
    (base 10) number 13 is
    A. 1011   B. 1010   C. 1101   D. 1100   E. none of these

15. The decimal (base 10) symbol equivalent to the binary (base   15.____
    2) number 11101 is
    A. 13   B. 24   C. 19   D. 30   E. none of these

16. The hexadecimal (base 16) symbol equivalent to the decimal   16.____
    (base 10) number 2605 is
    A. A2D   B. 3402
    C. 101000101101   D. B6C
    E. none of the above

17. The hexadecimal ____ symbol equivalent to the decimal   17.____
    (base 10) number 59 is
    A. 4A   B. A4   C. 3B   D. B3   E. none of these

18. The binary (base 2) symbol equivalent to the hexadecimal 18.___
    value 4D3CE is
    A. 01000000111101010000   B. 00110101110010110001
    C. 10001101110010001100   D. 01001101001111001110
    E. none of the above

19. The hexadecimal (base 16) symbol equivalent to the binary 19.___
    (base 2) number 100010011010 is
    A. 82C   B. 74   C. AC1   D. 89A   E. none of these

20. The octal (base 8) symbol equivalent to the binary (base 2) 20.___
    number 101111011001 is
    A. BD9   B. 42   C. 18   D. 5731   E. none of these

21. Consider the following input data: John, O Reilly, Johnson, 21.___
    O'Reilly.
    If a computer were to arrange these names according to
    the standard collating sequence, the output would be
    A. Johnson, John, O Reilly, O'Reilly
    B. John, Johnson, O'Reilly, O Reilly
    C. O'Reilly, O Reilly, Johnson, John
    D. John, Johnson, O Reilly, O'Reilly
    E. both a or c

22. In reference to the diagram below, this flowchart sequence 22.___
    describes
    A. conditional flow   B. branching
    C. repetitive flow   D. logical flow
    E. sequential flow

```
+-----------+
|  step 1   |
+-----------+
      |
      v
+-----------+
|  step 2   |
+-----------+
      |
      v
+-----------+
|  step 3   |
+-----------+
```

23. Which of the following comparisons would result in a true 23.___
    outcome?
    A. 5 = 10 or 6 = 5 and 8 = 2
    B. 10 = 12 and 6 = 6
    C. 7 = 4 or 9 = 9 and 4 = 4
    D. 5 = 5 and 3 = 2 or 7 = 7
    E. none of the above

24. Which of the following comparisons would result in a true 24.___
    outcome?
    A. 5 > 6 and 8 > 4
    B. 5 > 6 or 4 > 8
    C. 10 = 10 and 8 < 4 or 8 < 3
    D. 67 = 67 and 101 < 345 or 3 = 9
    E. none of the above

25. Which of the following comparisons would result in a
    true outcome?
    A. 5 = 6 or 7 < 3
    B. (10 < 12 or 14 = 15) and 9 = 9
    C. (17 > 10 or 5 < 6) and 5 > 7
    D. 88 < = 88 and 99 < 98
    E. none of the above

_____

KEY (CORRECT ANSWERS)

1.	B		11.	B
2.	E		12.	A
3.	C		13.	C
4.	B		14.	C
5.	C		15.	E
6.	B		16.	A
7.	D		17.	C
8.	A		18.	D
9.	B		19.	D
10.	D		20.	D

21. D
22. E
23. C
24. D
25. B

_____

EXAMINATION SECTION

DIRECTIONS: Each question or incomplete statement is followed by several suggested answers or completions. Select the one that BEST answers the question or completes the statement. *PRINT THE LETTER OF THE CORRECT ANSWER IN THE SPACE AT THE RIGHT.*

TEST 1

Questions 1-7.

DIRECTIONS: Questions 1 through 7 are to be answered SOLELY on the basis of the following passage.

The first step in establishing a programming development schedule is to rate the programs to be developed or to be maintained on the basis of complexity, size, and input-output complexity. The most experienced programmer should rate the program complexity based on the system flow chart. The same person should do all of the rating so that all programs are rated in the same manner. If possible, the same person who rates the complexity should estimate the program size based on the number of pages of coding. This rating can easily be checked, after coding has been completed, against the number of pages of coding actually produced. If there is consistent error in the estimates for program size, all future estimates should be corrected for this error or the estimating method reviewed.

The input-output rating is a mechanical count of the number of input and output units or tapes which the program uses. The objective is to measure the number of distinct files which the program must control.

After the ratings have been completed, the man-days required for each of the tasks can be calculated. Good judgment or, if available, a table of past experience is used to translate the ratings into man-days, the units in which the schedule is expressed. The calculations should keep the values for each task completely separate so that a later evaluation can be made by program, programmer, and function.

After the values have been calculated, it is a simple matter to establish a development schedule. This can be a simple bar chart which assigns work to specific programmers, a complex computer program using the *PERT* technique of critical path scheduling, or other useful type of document.

1. The rating and estimating of the programs should be performed by   1.___
   A. the person who will do the programming
   B. a programmer trainee
   C. the most experienced programmer
   D. the operations supervisor

2. The measurement used to express the programming schedule   2.___
   is the number of
   A. distinct files controlled by the programmer
   B. man-days
   C. pages of coding
   D. programmers

3. A mechanical count of the number of input and output units   3.___
   or tapes should be considered as a(n)
   A. input-output rating
   B. measure of the number of man-days required
   C. rating of complexity
   D. estimate of the number of pages of coding

4. Programming development scheduling methods are for   4.___
   A. new programs only
   B. programs to be developed and maintained
   C. large and complicated programs only
   D. maintenance programs only

5. If there is a consistent error in the estimates for program   5.___
   size, all estimates should be
   A. adjusted for future programs
   B. eliminated for all programs
   C. replaced by rating of complexity
   D. replaced by input-output rating

6. It is intimated that   6.___
   A. the calculations should keep the valuations for each
      task completely separated
   B. it is a simple matter to establish a development
      schedule
   C. the man-days required for each of the tasks can be
      calculated
   D. a later evaluation will be made

7. Complexity of programs can be checked   7.___
   A. before coding has been completed
   B. after future estimates have been corrected for error
   C. as a first step in establishing a complex computer
      program
   D. with reference to the number of pages of coding produced

Questions 8-13.

DIRECTIONS: Questions 8 through 13 are to be answered SOLELY on the
            basis of the following passage.

   The purposes of program testing are to determine that the program
has been coded correctly, that the coding matches the logical design,
and that the logical design matches the basic requirements of the job
as set down in the specifications. Program errors fall into the
following categories: errors in logic, clerical errors, misidentifica-
tion of the computer components' functions, misinterpretation of the
requirements of the job, and system analysis errors.

The number of errors in a program will average one for each 125 instructions, assuming that the programmer has been reasonably careful in his coding system. The number of permutations and combinations of conditions in a program may reach into the billions before each possibility has been thoroughly checked out. It is, therefore, a practical impossibility to check out each and every possible combination of conditions - the effort would take years, even in the simplest program. As a result, it is quite possible for errors to remain latent for a number of years, suddenly appearing when a particular combination is reached which had not previously occurred.

Latent program errors will remain in operating programs, and their occurrence should be minimized by complete and thorough testing. The fact that the program is operative and reaches end-of-job satisfactorily does not mean that all of the exception conditions and their permutations and combinations have been tested. Quite the contrary, many programs reach end-of-job after very few tests, since the *straight-line* part of the program is often simplest. However, the exceptions programmed to deal with a minimal percentage of the input account for a large percentage of the instructions. It is, therefore, quite possible to reach the end-of-job halt with only 10% of the program checked out.

8. One of the MAIN points of this passage is that   8.___
   A. it is impossible to do a good job of programming
   B. reaching end-of-job means only 10% of the program is checked out
   C. standard testing procedures should require testing of every possible combination of conditions
   D. elimination of all errors can never be assured, but the occurrence of errors can be minimized by thorough testing

9. Latent program errors GENERALLY   9.___
   A. evade detection for some time
   B. are detected in the last test run
   C. test the number of permutations and combinations in a program
   D. allow the program to go to end-of-job

10. Which one of the following statements pertaining to errors 10.___
    in a program is CORRECT?
    A. If the program has run to a normal completion, then all program errors have been eliminated.
    B. Program errors, if not caught in testing, will surely be detected in the first hundred runs of the program.
    C. It is practically impossible to verify that the typical program is free of errors.
    D. A program that is coded correctly is free of errors.

11. Among other things, program testing is designed to   11.___
    A. assure that the documentation is correct
    B. assure that the coding is correct
    C. determine the program running time
    D. measure programmer's performance

12. The difficulty in detecting errors in programs is due to   12.___
    A. the extremely large number of conditions that exist
       in a program
    B. poor analysis of work errors
    C. very sophisticated and clever programming
    D. reaching the end-of-job halt with only 10% of the
       program checked out

13. If the program being tested finally reaches the end-of-job   13.___
    halt, it means that
    A. one path through the program has been successfully
       tested
    B. less than 10% of the program has been tested
    C. the program has been coded correctly
    D. the logical design is correct

Questions 14-20.

DIRECTIONS: Questions 14 through 20 are to be answered SOLELY on
                the basis of the following passage.

Systems analysis represents a major link in the chain of trans-
lations from the problem to its machine solution. After the problem
and its requirements for solution have been stated in clear terms,
the systems analyst defines the broad outlines of the machine solution. He must know the overall capabilities of the equipment, and
he must be familiar with the application. The ultimate output of
the analysis is a detailed job specification containing all the tools
necessary to produce a series of computer programs. The purpose of
the specifications is to document and describe the system by defining
the problem and the proposed solution, explain system outputs and
functions, state system requirements for programmers, and to avoid
misunderstandings among involved departments. The specification
serves as a link between the analysis of the problem and the next
function, programming. Systems analysis relies on creativity rather
than rote analysis to develop effective computer systems. But this
creativity must be channeled and documented effectively if lasting
value is to be obtained.

14. According to the above paragraph, the systems analyst MUST 14.___
    be familiar with
    A. programming and the machine solution
    B. the machine solution and the next function
    C. the application and programming
    D. the application and the equipment capabilities

15. According to the above paragraph, the time that systems   15.___
    analysis MUST be performed is
    A. *after* the problem analysis
    B. *after* programming
    C. *before* problem definition
    D. *before* problem analysis

16. According to the above paragraph, the MAIN task performed   16.___
    by the systems analyst is to
    A. write the program
    B. analyze the problem
    C. define the overall capacities of the equipment
    D. define the machine solution of the problem

17. According to the above paragraph, the document produced   17.___
    by the systems analyst as his main output does NOT normally
    include
    A. an explanation of system outputs
    B. system requirements for programmers
    C. a statement of the problem
    D. performance standards

18. According to the above paragraph, the systems analysis   18.___
    function is
    A. relatively straightforward, requiring little creative
       effort
    B. extremely complex, making standard procedures impossible
    C. primarily a rote memory procedure
    D. a creative effort

19. According to the above paragraph, the specification   19.___
    A. is a major link in the sequence from problem to
       machine solution
    B. states the problem and its requirements for solution
    C. is chiefly concerned with the overall capabilities
       of the equipment
    D. represents the ultimate product of systems analysis

20. According to the above paragraph, the sequential function   20.___
    after the analysis of the program is
    A. documentation   B. application
    C. definition   D. programming

Questions 21-25.

DIRECTIONS: Questions 21 through 25 are to be answered SOLELY on
              the basis of the following passage.

Currently, memory represents one of the main limitations on
computer performance and, as a result, is one of the areas where
technological improvements will prove most fruitful.

Historically, the main problem of computer memories has been a
very unfavorable cost-to-speed ratio. Memory devices which have great
speed cost disproportionately more than those with less speed. This
problem has forced computer designers to use minimum amounts of rapid
access memory and to rely mainly on slower, large capacity storage.
This practice has resulted in a *memory tree*, where a hierarchy of
memory devices provides various increments of storage at different
costs and speeds for various purposes.

To achieve better speed/cost ratios, designers are increasingly turning to memory media other than the traditional ferrite cores. These cores now account for over 90% of the memory market. Plated wire and semiconductors are the media most likely to supplant ferrite cores. Semiconductors are expected to rapidly displace cores, starting with higher speed memories. Their costs are dropping sharply and are expected to drop as much as five-fold by the middle of this decade, while their speeds are at least doubling.

Despite the increasing use of competing technologies, ferrite cores will probably still dominate the extended random access storage area. Since the largest increment of storage is associated with ferrite core memory devices, their share of the internal memory market was well over 50% by 1980. The only factor militating against this is the possibility that the largest manufacturers of computers may abandon the extended internal storage concept.

Memory developments likely to happen later in this decade include the progressive replacement of magnetic drums by magnetic disks. The latter were themselves displaced near the end of the seventies by electrooptical units, followed by magnetic bubble storage. It also may prove possible to show the feasibility of associative processors. Under this concept, which is still experimental, data access would be considerably speeded through use of Contents-Addressable-Memories (CAM).

21. According to the above passage, a hierarchy of memory   21.___
    devices which provides various increments of storage at
    different costs and speeds has been used by designers
    because
       A. one of the larger manufacturers of computers might
          abandon the extended internal storage concept
       B. of the very unfavorable cost-to-speed ratio of
          computer memories
       C. magnetic disks have progressively replaced magnetic
          drums in the mid-seventies
       D. data access is expected to be appreciably speeded up
          through the use of Content-Addressable-Memories

22. According to the above passage, which of the following   22.___
    memory developments is MOST likely to have occurred by
    1980?
       A. Designers will turn to memories other than core for
          90% of their needs.
       B. Cores and semiconductors will largely replace plated
          wire memories.
       C. Cores and semiconductors will largely be replaced by
          electrooptical and magnetic bubble storage.
       D. Ferrite core will continue to dominate the internal
          memory market.

23. According to the above passage, the speed/cost ratio for   23.___
    semiconductors is
       A. becoming more favorable
       B. the same as the speed/cost ratio for plated wire

6

      C. remaining constant
      D. less favorable than the speed/cost ratio for ferrite
         core

24. According to the information in the passage, development   24.___
    of improved memory technology is IMPORTANT because
      A. it demonstrates the feasibility of associative
         processors
      B. memory represents one of the chief limitations on
         computer performance today
      C. semiconductors are expected to largely replace core
         which now represents about half of the memory market
      D. data can now be speeded through the use of CAM

25. Three types of memory media which are discussed in the   25.___
    above passage are
      A. core, plated wire, semiconductors
      B. high speed buffer, magnetic disks, rotating magnetic
         storage
      C. ferrite cores, magnetic drums, remote data terminals
      D. high speed buffers, magnetic disks, magnetic drums

TEST 2

Questions 1-5.

DIRECTIONS: Questions 1 through 5 are to be answered SOLELY on the
             basis of the following paragraph.

    Work standards presuppose an ability to measure work. Measurement
in office management is needed for several reasons. First, it is
necessary to evaluate the overall efficiency of the office itself. It
is then essential to measure the efficiency of each particular section
or unit and that of the individual worker. To plan and control the
work of sections and units, one must have measurement. A program of
measurement goes hand in hand with a program of standards. One can
have measurement without standards, but one cannot have work standards
without measurement. Providing data on amount of work done and time
expended, measurement does not deal with the amount of energy expended
by an individual although, in many cases, such energy may be in direct
proportion to work output. Usually from two-thirds to three-fourths
of all work can be measured. However, less than two-thirds of all
work is actually measured because measurement difficulties are
encountered when office work is non-repetitive and irregular, or when
it is primarily mental rather than manual. These obstacles are often
used as excuses for non-measurement far more frequently than is
justified.

1. According to the above paragraph, an office manager cannot   1.___
   set work standards unless he can
   A. plan the amount of work to be done
   B. control the amount of work that is done
   C. estimate accurately the quantity of work done
   D. delegate the amount of work to be done to efficient
      workers

2. According to the above paragraph, the type of office work   2.___
   that would be MOST difficult to measure would be
   A. checking warrants for accuracy of information
   B. recording payroll changes
   C. processing applications
   D. making up a new system of giving out supplies

3. According to the above paragraph, the ACTUAL amount of work   3.___
   that is measured is _____ of all work.
   A. less than two-thirds
   B. two-thirds to three-fourths
   C. less than three-sixths
   D. more than three-fourths

4. Which of the following would be MOST difficult to deter-   4.___
   mine by using measurement techniques?
   A. The amount of work that is accomplished during a
      certain period of time
   B. The amount of work that should be planned for a
      period of time
   C. How much time is needed to do a certain task
   D. The amount of incentive a person must have to do his
      job

5. The one of the following which is the MOST suitable title   5.___
   for the above paragraph is
   A. HOW MEASUREMENT OF OFFICE EFFICIENCY DEPENDS ON WORK
      STANDARDS
   B. USING MEASUREMENT FOR OFFICE MANAGEMENT AND EFFICIENCY
   C. WORK STANDARDS AND THE EFFICIENCY OF THE OFFICE WORKER
   D. MANAGING THE OFFICE USING MEASURED WORK STANDARDS

Questions 6-9.

DIRECTIONS: Questions 6 through 9 are to be answered SOLELY on the
              basis of the following passage.

Work measurement concerns accomplishment or productivity. It
has to do with results; it does not deal with the amount of energy
used up, although in many cases this may be in direct proportion to
the work output. Work measurement not only helps a manager to dis-
tribute work loads fairly, but it also enables him to define work
success in actual units, evaluate employee performance, and determine
where corrective help is needed. Work measurement is accomplished by
measuring the amount produced, measuring the time spent to produce it,
and relating the two. To illustrate, it is common to speak of so

many orders processed within a given time. The number of orders processed becomes meaningful when related to the amount of time taken.

Much of the work in an office can be measured fairly accurately and inexpensively. The extent of work measurement possible in any given case will depend upon the particular type of office tasks performed, but usually from two-thirds to three-fourths of all work in an office can be measured. It is true that difficulty in work measurement is encountered, for example, when the office work is irregular and not repeated often, or when the work is primarily mental rather than manual. These are problems, but they are used as excuses for doing no work measurement far more frequently than is justified.

6. According to the above passage, which of the following   6.___
   BEST illustrates the type of information obtained as a
   result of work measurement?
   A
   A. clerk takes one hour to file 150 folders
   B. typist types five letters
   C. stenographer works harder typing from shorthand notes
      than she does typing from a typed draft
   D. clerk keeps track of employees' time by computing sick
      leave, annual leave, and overtime leave

7. The above passage does NOT indicate that work measurement   7.___
   can be used to help a supervisor to determine
   A. *why* an employee is performing poorly on the job
   B. *who* are the fast and slow workers in the unit
   C. *how* the work in the unit should be divided up
   D. *how* long it should take to perform a certain task

8. According to the above passage, the kind of work that   8.___
   would be MOST difficult to measure would be such work as
   A. sorting mail
   B. designing a form for a new procedure
   C. photocopying various materials
   D. answering inquiries with form letters

9. The excuses mentioned in the above passage for failure to   9.___
   perform work measurement can be BEST summarized as the
   A. repetitive nature of office work
   B. costs involved in carrying out accurate work measurement
   C. inability to properly use the results obtained from work
      measurement
   D. difficulty involved in measuring certain types of work

Questions 10-13.

DIRECTIONS: Questions 10 through 13 are to be answered SOLELY on the
            basis of the following passage.

Job analysis combined with performance appraisal is an excellent method of determining training needs of individuals. The steps in this method are to determine the specific duties of the job, to evaluate the adequacy with which the employee performs each of these duties, and finally to determine what significant improvements can be made by training.

The list of duties can be obtained in a number of ways: asking the employee, asking the supervisor, observing the employee, etc. Adequacy of performance can be estimated by the employee, but the supervisor's evaluation must also be obtained. This evaluation will usually be based on observation.

What does the supervisor observe? The employee, while he is working; the employee's work relationships; the ease, speed, and sureness of the employee's actions; the way he applies himself to the job; the accuracy and amount of completed work, its conformity with established procedures and standards; the appearance of the work; the soundness of judgment it shows; and, finally, signs of good or poor communication, understanding, and cooperation among employees.

Such observation is a normal and inseparable part of the every-day job of supervision. Systematically recorded, evaluated, and summarized, it highlights both general and individual training needs.

10. According to the above passage, job analysis may be used   10.___
    by the supervisor in
    A. increasing his own understanding of tasks performed
       in his unit
    B. increasing efficiency of communication within the
       organization
    C. assisting personnel experts in the classification of
       positions
    D. determining in which areas an employee needs more
       instruction

11. According to the above passage, the FIRST step in deter-   11.___
    mining the training needs of employees is to
    A. locate the significant improvements that can be made
       by training
    B. determine the specific duties required in a job
    C. evaluate the employee's performance
    D. motivate the employee to want to improve himself

12. On the basis of the above passage, which of the following   12.___
    is the BEST way for a supervisor to determine the adequacy
    of employee performance?
    A. Check the accuracy and amount of completed work
    B. Ask the training officer
    C. Observe all aspects of the employee's work
    D. Obtain the employee's own estimate

13. Which of the following is NOT mentioned by the above   13.___
    passage as a factor to be taken into consideration in
    judging the adequacy of employee performance?
    A. Accuracy of completed work
    B. Appearance of completed work
    C. Cooperation among employees
    D. Attitude of the employee toward his supervisor

Questions 14-15.

DIRECTIONS: Questions 14 and 15 are to be answered SOLELY on the
              basis of the following paragraph.

The fundamental characteristic of the type of remote control
which management needs to bridge the gap between itself and actual
operations is the more effective use of records and reports - more
specifically, the gathering and interpretation of the facts con-
tained in records and reports. Facts, for management purposes, are
those data (narrative and quantitative) which express in simple terms
the current standing of the agency's program, work, and resources in
relation to the plans and policies formulated by management. They
are those facts or measures (1) which permit management to compare
current status with past performance and with its forecasts for the
immediate future, and (2) which provide management with a reliable
basis for long-range forecasting.

14.   For management purposes, facts are, according to the above   14.___
      paragraph,
         A. forecasts which can be compared to current status
         B. data which can be used for certain control purposes
         C. a fundamental characteristic of a type of remote control
         D. the data contained in records and reports

15.   An inference which can be drawn from this statement is   15.___
      that
         A. management which has a reliable basis for long-range
            forecasting has at its disposal a type of remote con-
            trol which is needed to bridge the gap between itself
            and actual operations
         B. data which do not express in simple terms the current
            standing of the agency's program, work, and resources
            in relationship to the plans and policies formulated
            by management may still be facts for management
            purposes
         C. data which express relationships among the agency's
            program, work, and resources are management facts
         D. the gap between management and actual operations can
            only be bridged by characteristics which are funda-
            mentally a type of remote control

Questions 16-17.

DIRECTIONS: Questions 16 and 17 are to be answered SOLELY on the
              basis of the following passage.

Two approaches are available in developing criteria for the
evaluation of plans. One approach, designated Approach A, is a review
and analysis of characteristics that differentiate successful plans
from unsuccessful plans. These criteria are descriptive in nature
and serve as a checklist against which the plan under consideration
may be judged. These characteristics have been observed by many
different students of planning, and there is considerable agreement
concerning the characteristics necessary for a plan to be successful.

A second approach to the development of criteria for judging plans, designated Approach B, is the determination of the degree to which the plan under consideration is economic. The word *economic* is used here in its broadest sense; i.e., effective in its utilization of resources. In order to determine the economic worth of a plan, it is necessary to use a technique that permits the description of any plan in economic terms and to utilize this technique to the extent that it becomes a *way of thinking* about plans.

16. According to Approach B, the MOST successful plan is   16.___
   generally one which
   A. costs least to implement
   B. gives most value for resources expended
   C. uses the least expensive resources
   D. utilizes the greatest number of resources

17. According to Approach A, a successful plan is one which is 17.___
   A. descriptive in nature
   B. lowest in cost
   C. similar to other successful plans
   D. agreed upon by many students of planning

Questions 18-20.

DIRECTIONS: Questions 18 through 20 are to be answered SOLELY on the basis of the following passage.

The primary purpose of control reports is to supply information intended to serve as the basis for corrective action if needed. At the same time, the significance of control reports must be kept in proper perspective. Control reports are only a part of the planning-management information system. Control information includes non-financial as well as financial data that measure performance and isolate variances from standard. Control information also provides feedback so that planning information may be updated and corrected. Whenever possible, control reports should be designed so that they provide feedback for the planning process as well as provide information of immediate value to the control process.

Since the culmination of the control process is the taking of necessary corrective action to bring performance in line with standards, it follows that control information must be directed to the person who is organizationally responsible for taking the required action. Usually the same information, though in a somewhat abbreviated form, is given to the responsible manager's superior. A district sales manager needs a complete daily record of the performance of each of his salesmen; yet, the report forwarded to the regional sales manager summarizes only the performance of each sales district in his region. In preparing reports for higher echelons of management, summary statements and recommendations for action should appear on the first page; substantiating data, usually the information presented to the person directly responsible for the operation, may be included if needed.

18. A control report serves its primary purpose as part of the   18.___
process which leads DIRECTLY to
    A. better planning for future action
    B. increasing the performance of district salesmen
    C. the establishment of proper performance standards
    D. taking corrective action when performance is poor

19. The one of the following which would be the BEST descrip-   19.___
tion of a control report is that a control report is a
form of
    A. planning   B. communication
    C. direction   D. organization

20. If control reports are to be effective, the one of the   20.___
following which is LEAST essential to the effectiveness
of control reporting is a system of
    A. communication   B. standards
    C. authority   D. work simplification

Questions 21-23.

DIRECTIONS: Questions 21 through 23 are to be answered SOLELY on
the basis of the following passage.

The need for the best in management techniques has given rise to
the expression *scientific management*. Within reasonable limits,
management can be scientific, but it will probably be many decades
before it becomes truly scientific either in the factory or in the
office. As long as it is impossible to measure accurately individual
performance and to equate human behavior, so long will it be impossible
to develop completely scientific techniques of office management.
There is a likelihood, of course, that management might be reduced to
a science when it is applied to inanimate objects which facilitate
operations such as machinery, office equipment and furnishings, and
forms. The limiting factor, therefore, is the human element.

21. The above passage is concerned PRIMARILY with the   21.___
    A. value of scientific office management
    B. methods for the development of scientific office
       management
    C. need for the best office management techniques
    D. possibility of reducing office management to a science

22. According to the above passage, the realization of truly   22.___
scientific office management is dependent upon the
    A. expression of management techniques
    B. development of accurate personnel measurement techniques
    C. passage of many decades, most probably
    D. elimination of individual differences in human behavior

23. According to the above passage, the scientific management   23.___
of inanimate objects
    A. occurs automatically because there is no human factor
    B. cannot occur in a factory, but can occur in an office

      C. could be achieved without the concurrent achievement
         of truly scientific office management
      D. is not a necessary component of truly scientific
         office management

Questions 24-25.

DIRECTIONS: Questions 24 and 25 are to be answered SOLELY on the
             basis of the following paragraph.

    Your role as human resources utilization experts is to submit
your techniques to operating administrators, for the program must,
in reality, be theirs, not yours. We, in personnel, have been guilty
of encouraging operating executives to believe that these important
matters affecting their employees are personnel department matters,
not management matters. We should hardly be surprised, as a conse-
quence, to find these executives playing down the role of personnel
and finding personnel *routines* a nuisance, for these are not in the
mainstream of managing the enterprise - or so we have encouraged them
to believe.

24.   The BEST of the following interpretations of the above   24.___
     paragraph is that
      A. personnel people have been guilty of *passing the buck*
         on personnel functions
      B. operating officials have difficulty understanding
         personnel techniques
      C. personnel employees have tended to usurp some functions
         rightfully belonging to management
      D. matters affecting employees should be handled by the
         personnel department

25.   The BEST of the following interpretations of the above   25.___
     paragraph is that
      A. personnel departments have aided and abetted the
         formulation of negative attitudes on the part of
         management
      B. personnel people are labor relations experts and
         should carry out these duties
      C. personnel activities are not really the responsibility
         of management
      D. management is now being encouraged by personnel experts
         to assume some responsibility for personnel functions

TEST 3

Questions 1-3.

DIRECTIONS: Questions 1 through 3 are to be answered SOLELY on the basis of the following paragraph.

Prior to revising its child care program, a department feels that it is necessary to get some information from the mothers served by the existing program in order to determine where changes are required. A questionnaire is to be constructed to obtain this information.

1. Of the following points which can be taken into considera-
   tion in the construction of the questionnaire, the one
   which is of LEAST importance is
   A. that the data are to be put into punch cards
   B. the aspects of the program which seem to be in need of
      change
   C. the type of person who will fill out the questionnaire
   D. testing the questionnaire for ambiguity in advance of
      general distribution
   E. setting up a control group so that answers received
      can be compared to a standard

   1.___

2. To discuss this questionnaire with all mothers who have
   been asked to answer it, before they actually fill it out,
   is
   A. *desirable*; the mothers may be able to offer valuable
      suggestions for changes in the form of the questionnaire
   B. *undesirable*; it is of some value but consumes too much
      valuable time
   C. *desirable*; cooperation and uniform interpretation will
      tend to be achieved
   D. *undesirable*; it may cause the answers to be biased
   E. *desirable*; the group will tend to support the program

   2.___

3. Of the following items included in the questionnaire, the
   one which will be of LEAST assistance for comparing
   attitudes toward the program among different kinds of
   persons is
   A. name   B. address   C. age
   D. place of birth E. education

   3.___

Questions 4-6.

DIRECTIONS: Questions 4 through 6 are to be answered SOLELY on the basis of the following paragraph.

The supervisor of a large clerical and statistical division has assigned to one of the units under his supervision the preparation of a special statistical report required by the department head. The unit head accepted the assignment without comment but soon ran into considerable difficulty because no one in his unit had had any statistical training.

4. If a result of this lack of training is that the report is
not completed on time, although everyone has done all that
could be expected, the responsibility for the failure rests
with

    A. the department head   B. the supervisor
    C. the unit head   D. the employees in the unit
    E. no one

4.__

5. This incident indicates that the supervisory staff has
insufficient knowledge of employee

    A. capabilities
    B. reaction to increased demands
    C. on-the-job training needs
    D. work habits
    E. ability to perform ordinary assignments

5.__

6. After working on the report for two days, the unit head
notifies the supervisor that he will not be able to get the
report out in the required time. He states that his staff
will be completely trained in another day or two and that
after that preparing the report will be a simple matter.
At this stage, the supervisor decides to have the statistical unit prepare the report.
This action on the part of the supervisor is

    A. *undesirable*; the unit head should be given an incentive
        to continue with his training program which may produce
        good results
    B. *desirable*; it is the most effective way in which the
        supervisor can show his displeasure with the unit
        head's failure
    C. *undesirable*; it may adversely affect the morale of the
        unit
    D. *desirable*; it will generally result in a better report
        completed in a shorter time
    E. *undesirable*; the time spent on training the unit will
        be completely wasted

6.__

Questions 7-9.

DIRECTIONS: Questions 7 through 9 are to be answered SOLELY on
the basis of the following paragraph.

The regressive uses of discipline are ubiquitous. Administrative
architects who seek the optimum balance between structure and morale
must accordingly look toward the identification and isolation of
disciplinary elements. The whole range of disciplinary sanctions,
from the reprimand to the dismissal, presents opportunities for
reciprocity and accommodation of institutional interests. When
rightly seized upon, these opportunities may provide the moment and
the means for fruitful exercise of leadership and collaboration.

7. The one of the following ways of reworking the ideas
presented in the above paragraph in order to be BEST
suited for presentation in an in-service training course
in supervision is:

7.__

A. When one of your men does something wrong, talk it over with him. Tell him what he should have done. This is a chance for you to show the man that you are on his side and that you would welcome him on your side.
B. It is not necessary to reprimand or to dismiss an employee because he needs disciplining. The alert foreman will lead and collaborate with his subordinates, making discipline unnecessary.
C. A good way to lead the men you supervise is to take those opportunities which present themselves to use the whole range of disciplinary sanctions from reprimand to dismissal as a means for enforcing collaboration.
D. Chances to punish a man in your squad should be welcomed as opportunities to show that you are a *good guy* who does not bear a grudge.
E. Before you talk to a man or have him report to the office for something he has done wrong, attempt to lead him and get him to work with you. Tell him that his actions were wrong, that you expect him not to repeat the same wrong act, and that you will take a firmer stand if the act is repeated.

8. Of the following, the PRINCIPAL point made in the paragraph 8.___
   above is that
   A. discipline is frequently used improperly
   B. it is possible to isolate the factors entering into a disciplinary situation
   C. identification of the disciplinary elements is desirable
   D. disciplinary situations may be used to the advantage of the organization
   E. obtaining the best relationship between organizational form and spirit depends upon the ability to label disciplinary elements

9. The MOST novel idea presented in the above paragraph is 9.___
   that
   A. discipline is rarely necessary
   B. discipline may be a joint action of man and supervisor
   C. there are disciplinary elements which may be identified
   D. a range of disciplinary sanctions exists
   E. it is desirable to seek for balance between structure and morale.

Questions 10-11.

DIRECTIONS: Questions 10 and 11 are to be answered SOLELY on the basis of the following paragraph.

People must be selected to do the tasks involved and must be placed on a payroll in jobs fairly priced. Each of these people must be assigned those tasks which he can perform best; the work of each must be appraised, and good and poor work singled out appropriately. Skill in performing assigned tasks must be developed, and the total work situation must be conducive to sustained high performance. Finally, employees must be separated from the work force either voluntarily or involuntarily because of inefficient or unsatisfactory performance or because of curtailment of organizational activities.

10. A personnel function which is NOT included in the above   10.___
    description is
    A. classification   B. training   C. placement
    D. severance   E. service rating

11. The underlying implied purpose of the policy enunciated in   11.___
    the above paragraph is
    A. to plan for the curtailment of the organizational
       program when it becomes necessary
    B. to single out appropriate skill in performing assigned
       tasks
    C. to develop and maintain a high level of performance by
       employees
    D. that training employees in relation to the total work
       situation is essential if good and poor work are to be
       singled out
    E. that equal money for equal work results in a total work
       situation which insures proper appraisal

Questions 12-16.

DIRECTIONS: Questions 12 through 16 are to be answered SOLELY on
              the basis of the following sections which appeared in
              a report on the work production of two bureaus of a
              department.
              Throughout the report, assume that each month has 4 weeks.

    Each of the two bureaus maintains a chronological file. In
Bureau A, every 9 months on the average, this material fills a
standard legal size file cabinet sufficient for 12,000 work units.
In Bureau B, the same type of cabinet is filled in 18 months. Each
bureau maintains three complete years of information plus a current
file. When the current file cabinet is filled, the cabinet containing the oldest material is emptied, the contents disposed of, and
the cabinet used for current material. The similarity of these
operations makes it possible to consolidate these files with little
effort.

    Study of the practice of using typists as filing clerks for
periods when there is no typing work showed (1) Bureau A has for the
past 6 months completed a total of 1500 filing work units a week
using on the average 200 man-hours of trained file clerk time and
20 man-hours of typist time, (2) Bureau B has in the same period
completed a total of 2000 filing work units a week using on the
average 125 man-hours of trained file clerk time and 60 hours of
typist time. This includes all work in chronological files.
Assuming that all clerks work at the same speed and that all typists
work at the same speed, this indicates that work other than filing
should be found for typists or that they should be given some
training in the filing procedures used.... It should be noted that

18

Bureau A has not been producing the 1,600 units of technical (not filing) work per 30 day period required by Schedule K, but is at present 200 units behind. The Bureau should be allowed 3 working days to get on schedule.

12. What percentage (approximate) of the total number of   12.___
filing work units completed in both units consists of the
work involved in the maintenance of the chronological files?
A. 5%   B. 10%   C. 15%   D. 20%   E. 25%

13. If the two chronological files are consolidated, the   13.___
number of months which should be allowed for filling a
cabinet is
A. 2   B. 4   C. 6   D. 8   E. 14

14. The MAXIMUM number of file cabinets which can be released   14.___
for other uses as a result of the consolidation recommended
is
A. 0
B. 1
C. 2
D. 3
E. not determinable on the basis of the data given

15. If all the filing work for both units is consolidated   15.___
without any diminution in the amount to be done and all
filing work is done by trained file clerks, the number
of clerks required (35-hour work week) is
A. 4   B. 5   C. 6   D. 7   E. 8

16. In order to comply with the recommendation with respect   16.___
to Schedule K, the present work production of Bureau A
must be increased by
A. 50%
B. 100%
C. 150%
D. 200%
E. an amount which is not determinable on the basis of
the data given

Questions 17-18.

DIRECTIONS: Questions 17 and 18 are to be answered SOLELY on
the basis of the following paragraph.

Production planning is mainly a process of synthesis. As a basis
for the positive act of bringing complex production elements properly
together, however, analysis is necessary, especially if improvement is
to be made in an existing organization. The necessary analysis
requires customary means of orientation and preliminary fact gathering with emphasis, however, on the recognition of administrative
goals and of the relationship among work steps.

17. The entire process described is PRIMARILY one of   17.___
    A. taking apart, examining, and recombining
    B. deciding what changes are necessary, making the changes
       and checking on their value
    C. fact finding so as to provide the necessary orientation
    D. discovering just where the emphasis in production should
       be placed and then modifying the existing procedure so
       that it is placed properly
    E. recognizing administrative goals and the relationship
       among work steps

18. In production planning, according to the above paragraph,   18.___
    analysis is used PRIMARILY as
    A. a means of making important changes in an organization
    B. the customary means of orientation and preliminary fact
       finding
    C. a development of the relationship among work steps
    D. a means for holding the entire process intact by
       providing a logical basis
    E. a method to obtain the facts upon which a theory can
       be built

Questions 19-21.

DIRECTIONS: Questions 19 through 21 are to be answered SOLELY on
              the basis of the following paragraph.

    Public administration is policy-making. But it is not autonomous,
exclusive, or isolated policy-making. It is policy-making on a field
where mighty forces contend, forces engendered in and by society. It
is policy-making subject to still other and various policy makers.
Public administration is one of a number of basic political processes
by which these people achieve and control government.

19. From the point of view expressed in the above paragraph,   19.___
    public administration is
    A. becoming a technical field with completely objective
       processes
    B. the primary force in modern society
    C. a technical field which should be divorced from the
       actual decision-making function
    D. basically anti-democratic
    E. intimately related to politics

20. According to the above paragraph, public administration   20.___
    is NOT entirely
    A. a force generated in and by society
    B. subject at times to controlling influences
    C. a social process
    D. policy-making relating to administrative practices
    E. related to policy-making at lower levels

21. The above paragraph asserts that public administration   21.___
    A. develops the basic and controlling policies
    B. is the result of policies made by many different
       forces
    C. should attempt to break through its isolated policy-
       making and engage on a broader field
    D. is a means of directing government
    E. is subject to the political processes by which acts
       are controlled

Questions 22-24.

DIRECTIONS: Questions 22 through 24 are to be answered SOLELY on
the basis of the following paragraph.

In order to understand completely the source of an employee's
insecurity on his job, it is necessary to understand how he came to
be, who he is, and what kind of a person he is away from his job.
This would necessitate an understanding of those personal assets and
liabilities which the employee brings to the job situation. These
arise from his individual characteristics and his past experiences
and established patterns of interpersonal relations. This whole area
is of tremendous scope, encompassing everything included within the
study of psychiatry and interpersonal relations. Therefore, it has
been impracticable to consider it in detail. Attention has been
focused on the relatively circumscribed area of the actual occupation-
al situation. The factors considered - those which the employee
brings to the job situation and which arise from his individual
characteristics and his past experience and established patterns of
interpersonal relations - are: intellectual level or capacity,
specific aptitudes, education, work experience, health, social and
economic background, patterns of interpersonal relations and
resultant personality characteristics.

22. According to the above paragraph, the one of the following 22.___
    fields of study which would be of LEAST importance in the
    study of the problem is the
    A. relationships existing among employees
    B. causes of employee insecurity in the job situation
    C. conflict, if it exists, between intellectual level and
       work experience
    D. distribution of intellectual achievement
    E. relationship between employee characteristics and the
       established pattern of interpersonal relations in the
       work situation

23. According to the above paragraph, in order to make a   23.___
    thoroughgoing and comprehensive study of the sources of
    employee insecurity, the field of study should include
    A. only such circumscribed areas as are involved in
       extra-occupational situations
    B. a study of the dominant mores of the period
    C. all branches of the science of psychology

D. a determination of the characteristics, such as intellectual capacity, which an employee should bring to the job situation
E. employee personality characteristics arising from previous relationships with other people

24. It is implied by the above paragraph that it would be of GREATEST advantage to bring to this problem a comprehensive knowledge of

24.___

A. all established patterns of interpersonal relations
B. the milieu in which the employee group is located
C. what assets and liabilities are presented in the job situation
D. methods of focusing attention on relatively circumscribed regions
E. the sources of an employee's insecurity on his job

Questions 25-26.

DIRECTIONS: Questions 25 and 26 are to be answered SOLELY on the basis of the following paragraph.

If, during a study, some hundreds of values of a variable (such as annual number of latenesses for each employee in a department) have been noted merely in the arbitrary order in which they happen to occur, the mind cannot properly grasp the significance of the record; the observations must be ranked or classified in some way before the characteristics of the series can be comprehended, and those comparisons, on which arguments as to causation depend, can be made with other series. A dichotomous classification is too crude; if the values are merely classified according to whether they exceed or fall short of some fixed value, a large part of the information given by the original record is lost. Numerical measurements lend themselves with peculiar readiness to a manifold classification.

25. According to the above paragraph, if the values of a variable which are gathered during a study are classified in a few subdivisions, the MOST likely result will be

25.___

A. an inability to grasp the significance of the record
B. an inability to relate the series with other series
C. a loss of much of the information in the original data
D. a loss of the readiness with which numerical measurements lend themselves to a manifold classification
E. that the order in which they happen to occur will be arbitrary

26. The above paragraph advocates, with respect to numerical data, the use of

26.___

A. arbitrary order
B. comparisons with other series
C. a two value classification
D. a many value classification
E. all values of a variable

Question 27.

DIRECTIONS: Question 27 is to be answered SOLELY on the basis of
              the following paragraph.

A more significant manifestation of the concern of the community
with the general welfare is the collection and dissemination of
statistics. This statement may cause the reader to smile, for
statistics seem to be drab and prosaic things. The great growth of
statistics, however, is one of the most remarkable characteristics
of the age. Never before has a community kept track from month to
month, and in some cases from week to week, of how many people are
born, how many die and from what causes, how many are sick, how much
is being produced, how much is being sold, how many people are at
work, how many people are unemployed, how long they have been out of
work, what prices people pay, how much income they receive and from
what sources, how much they owe, what they intend to buy. These
elaborate attempts of the country to keep informed about what is
happening mean that the community is concerned with how its members
are faring and with the conditions under which they live. For this
reason, the present age may take pride in its numerous and regular
statistical reports and in the rapid increase in the number of these
reports. No other age has evidenced such a keen interest in the
conditions of the people.

27.   The writer implies that statistics are   27.___
      A. too scientific for general use
      B. too elaborate and too drab
      C. related to the improvement of living conditions
      D. frequently misinterpreted
      E. a product of the machine age

KEY (CORRECT ANSWERS)

TEST 1	TEST 2	TEST 3
1. C	1. C	1. E
2. B	2. D	2. C
3. A	3. A	3. A
4. B	4. D	4. B
5. A	5. B	5. A
6. D	6. A	6. D
7. D	7. A	7. A
8. D	8. B	8. D
9. A	9. D	9. B
10. C	10. D	10. A
11. B	11. B	11. C
12. A	12. C	12. C
13. A	13. D	13. C
14. D	14. B	14. B
15. A	15. C	15. D
16. D	16. B	16. E
17. D	17. C	17. A
18. D	18. D	18. E
19. D	19. B	19. E
20. D	20. D	20. D
21. B	21. D	21. D
22. D	22. B	22. D
23. A	23. C	23. E
24. B	24. C	24. B
25. A	25. A	25. C
		26. D
		27. C

CODING
EXAMINATION SECTION

COMMENTARY

An ingenious question-type called coding, involving elements of alpha-betizing, filing, name and number comparison, and evaluative judgment and application, has currently won wide acceptance in testing circles for measuring clerical aptitude and general ability, particularly on the senior (middle) grades (levels).

While the directions for this question usually vary in detail, the candidate is generally asked to consider groups of names, codes, and numbers, and, then, according to a given plan, to arrange codes in al-phabetic order; to arrange these in numerical sequence; to re-arrange columns of names and numbers in correct order; to espy errors in coding; to choose the correct coding arrangement in consonance with the given directions and examples, etc.

This question-type appears to have few paramaters in respect to form, substance, or degree of difficulty.

Accordingly, acquaintance with, and practice in, the coding question is recommended for the serious candidate.

———

EXAMINATION SECTION

TEST 1

DIRECTIONS FOR THIS SECTION:

	CODE TABLE
Name of Applicant	H A N G S B R U K E
Test Code	c o m p l e x i t y
File Number	0 1 2 3 4 5 6 7 8 9

Assume that each of the above *capital letters* is the first letter of the Name of an Applicant, that the *small letter* directly beneath each capital letter is the Test Code for the Applicant, and that the *number* directly beneath each code letter is the File Number for the Applicant.

In each of the following questions, the test code letters and the file numbers in Columns 2 and 3 should correspond to the capital letters in Column 1. For each question, look at each column carefully and mark your answer as follows:

If there is an error only in Column 2, mark your answer A.
If there is an error only in Column 3, mark your answer B.
If there is an error in both Columns 2 and 3, mark your answer C.
If both Columns 2 and 3 are correct, mark your answer D.

The following sample question is given to help you understand the procedure.

SAMPLE QUESTION

Column 1	Column 2	Column 3
AKEHN	otyci	18902

1

In Column 2, the final test code letter "i" should be "m." Column 3 is correctly coded to Column 1. Since there is an error only in Column 2, the answer is A.

	Column 1	Column 2	Column 3	
1.	NEKKU	mytti	29987	1. ...
2.	KRAEB	txlye	86095	2. ...
3.	ENAUK	ymoit	92178	3. ...
4.	REANA	xeomo	69121	4. ...
5.	EKHSE	ytcxy	97049	5. ...

TEST 2

DIRECTIONS FOR THIS SECTION: The employee identification codes in Column I begin and end with a capital letter and have an eight-digit number in between. In Questions 1 through 8, employee identification codes in Column I are to be arranged according to the following rules:

First: Arrange in alphabetical order according to the first letter.

Second: When two or more employee identification codes have the same first letter, arrange in alphabetical order according to the last letter.

Third: When two or more employee codes have the same first and last letters, arrange in numerical order beginning with the lowest number.

The employee identification codes in Column I are numbered 1 through 5 in the order in which they are listed. In Column II the numbers 1 through 5 are arranged in four different ways to show different arrangements of the corresponding employee identification numbers. Choose the answer in Column II in which the employee identification numbers are arranged according to the above rules.

SAMPLE QUESTION

Column I	Column II
1. E75044127B	A. 4, 1, 3, 2, 5
2. B96399104A	B. 4, 1, 2, 3, 5
3. B93939086A	C. 4, 3, 2, 5, 1
4. B47064465H	D. 3, 2, 5, 4, 1
5. B99040922A	

In the sample question, the four employee identification codes starting with B should be put before the employee identification code starting with E. The employee identification codes starting with B and ending with A should be put before the employee identification codes starting with B and ending with H. The three employee identification codes starting with B and ending with A should be listed in numerical order, beginning with the lowest number. The correct way to arrange the employee identification codes, therefore, is 3, 2, 5, 4, 1 shown below.

3. B93939086A
2. B96399104A
5. B99040922A
4. B47064465H
1. E75044127B

Therefore, the answer to the sample question is D. Now answer the following questions according to the above rules.

	Column I	Column II	
1.	1. G42786441J 2. H45665413J 3. G43117690J 4. G43546698I 5. G41679942I	A. 2, 5, 4, 3, 1 B. 5, 4, 1, 3, 2 C. 4, 5, 1, 3, 2 D. 1, 3, 5, 4, 2	1. ...
2.	1. S44556178T 2. T43457169T 3. S53321176T 4. T53317998S 5. S67673942S	A. 1, 3, 5, 2, 4 B. 4, 3, 5, 2, 1 C. 5, 3, 1, 2, 4 D. 5, 1, 3, 4, 2	2. ...
3.	1. R63394217D 2. R63931247D 3. R53931247D 4. R66874239D 5. R46799366D	A. 5, 4, 2, 3, 1 B. 1, 5, 3, 2, 4 C. 5, 3, 1, 2, 4 D. 5, 1, 2, 3, 4	3. ...
4.	1. A35671968B 2. A35421794C 3. A35466987B 4. C10435779A 5. C00634779B	A. 3, 2, 1, 4, 5 B. 2, 3, 1, 5, 4 C. 1, 3, 2, 4, 5 D. 3, 1, 2, 4, 5	4. ...
5.	1. I99746426Q 2. I10445311Q 3. J63749877P 4. J03421739Q 5. J00765311Q	A. 2, 1, 3, 5, 4 B. 5, 4, 2, 1, 3 C. 4, 5, 3, 2, 1 D. 2, 1, 4, 5, 3	5. ...
6.	1. M33964217N 2. N33942770N 3. N06155881M 4. M00433669M 5. M79034577N	A. 4, 1, 5, 2, 3 B. 5, 1, 4, 3, 2 C. 4, 1, 5, 3, 2 D. 1, 4, 5, 2, 3	6. ...
7.	1. D77643905C 2. D44106788C 3. D13976022F 4. D97655430E 5. D00439776F	A. 1, 2, 5, 3, 4 B. 5, 3, 2, 1, 4 C. 2, 1, 5, 3, 4 D. 2, 1, 4, 5, 3	7. ...
8.	1. W22746920A 2. W22743720A 3. W32987655A 4. W43298765A 5. W30987433A	A. 2, 1, 3, 4, 5 B. 2, 1, 5, 3, 4 C. 1, 2, 3, 4, 5 D. 1, 2, 5, 3, 4	8. ...

TEST 3

DIRECTIONS FOR THIS SECTION: Each of the following equestions consists of three sets of names and name codes. In each question, the two names and name codes on the same line are supposed to be exactly the same.

Look carefully at each set of names and codes and mark your answer:
    A. if there are mistakes in all three sets
    B. if there are mistakes in two of the sets
    C. if there is a mistake in only one set
    D. if there are no mistakes in any of the sets

3

SAMPLE QUESTION

The following sample question is given to help you understand the procedure.

Macabe, John N. - V 53162	Macade, John N. - V 53162
Howard, Joan S. - J 24791	Howard, Joan S. - J 24791
Ware, Susan B. - A 45068	Ware, Susan B. - A 45968

In the above sample question, the names and name codes of the first set are not exactly the same because of the spelling of the last name (Macabe - Macade). The names and name codes of the second set are exactly the same. The names and name codes of the third set are not exactly the same because the two name codes are different (A 45068 - A 45968). Since there are mistakes in only 2 of the sets, the answer to the sample question is B.

1. Powell, Michael C. - 78537 F   Powell, Michael C. - 78537 F   1. ...
   Martinez, Pablo,J. - 24435 P   Martinez, Pablo J. - 24435 P
   MacBane, Eliot M. - 98674 E   MacBane, Eliot M. - 98674 E
2. Fitz-Kramer Machines Inc.   Fitz-Kramer Machines Inc.   2. ...
                 - 259090   - 259090
   Marvel Cleaning Service   Marvel Cleaning Service
                 - 482657   - 482657
   Donato, Carl G.   - 637418   Danato, Carl G.   - 687418
3. Martin Davison Trading Corp.   Martin Davidson Trading Corp. 3. ...
                 - 43108 T   - 43108 T
   Cotwald Lighting Fixtures   Cotwald Lighting Fixtures
                 - 76065 L   - 70056 L
   R. Crawford Plumbers   R. Crawford Plumbers
                 - 23157 C   - 23157 G
4. Fraiman Engineering Corp.   Friaman Engineering Corp.   4. ...
                 - M4773   - M4773
   Neuman, Walter B. - N7745   Neumen, Walter B. - N7745
   Pierce, Eric M.   - W6304   Pierce, Eric M.   - W6304
5. Constable, Eugene - B 64837   Comstable, Eugene - B 64837 5. ...
   Derrick, Paul   - H 27119   Derrik, Paul   - H 27119
   Heller, Karen   - S 49606   Heller, Karen   - S 46906
6. Hernando Delivery Service   Hernando Delivery Service   6. ...
         Co. - D 7456   Co. - D 7456
   Barettz Electrical Supplies   Barettz Electrical Supplies
                 - N 5392   - N 5392
   Tanner, Abraham   - M 4798   Tanner, Abraham   - M 4798
7. Kalin Associates - R 38641   Kaline Associates - R 38641 7. ...
   Sealey, Robert E. - P 63533   Sealey, Robert E. - P 63553
   Scalsi Office Furniture   Scalsi Office Furniture
                 - R 36742   - R 36742
8. Janowsky, Philip M.- 742213   Janowsky, Philip M.- 742213 8. ...
   Hansen, Thomas H. - 934816   Hanson, Thomas H. - 934816
   L. Lester and Son Inc.   L. Lester and Son Inc.
                 - 294568   - 294568

TEST 4

DIRECTIONS FOR THIS SECTION: The following questions are to be answered on the basis of the following Code Table. In this table, for each number, a corresponding code letter is given. Each of the questions contains three pairs of numbers and code letters. In each pair, the code letters should correspond with the numbers in accordance with the Code Table.

CODE TABLE

Number	1	2	3	4	5	6	7	8	9	0
Corresponding Code Letter	Y	N	Z	X	W	T	U	P	S	R

In some of the pairs below, an error exists in the coding. Examine the pairs in each question carefully. If an error exists in:

Only one of the pairs in the question, mark your answer A.
Any two pairs in the question, mark your answer B.
All three pairs in the question, mark your answer C.
None of the pairs in the question, mark your answer D.

SAMPLE QUESTION

37258   - ZUNWP
948764 - SXPTTX
73196   - UZYSP

In the above sample, the first pair is correct since each number, as listed, has the correct corresponding code letter. In the second pair, an error exists because the number 7 should have the code letter U instead of the letter T. In the third pair, an error exists because the number 6 should have the code letter T instead of the letter P. Since there are errors in two of the three pairs, the correct answer is B.

1. 493785   - XSZUPW   1. ...
    86398207 - PTUSPNRU
    5943162   - WSXZYTN
2. 5413968412 - WXYZSTPXYR   2. ...
    8763451297 - PUTZXWYZSU
    4781965302 - XUPYSUWZRN
3. 79137584 - USYRUWPX   3. ...
    638247   - TZPNXS
    49679312 - XSTUSZYN
4. 37854296 - ZUPWXNST   4. ...
    09183298 - RSYXZNSP
    91762358 - SYUTNXWP
5. 3918762485 - ZSYPUTNXPW   5. ...
    1578291436 - YWUPNSYXZT
    2791385674 - NUSYZPWTUX
6. 197546821 - YSUWSTPNY   6. ...
    873024867 - PUZRNWPTU
    583179246 - WPZYURNXT
7. 510782463 - WYRUSNXTZ   7. ...
    478192356 - XUPYSNZWT
    961728532 - STYUNPWXN

TEST 5

CODING KEY

City Letter	P	J	R	T	Y	K	M	S	O
Code Number	1	2	3	4	5	6	7	8	9
Code Letter	a	b	c	d	e	f	g	h	i
Code Symbol	+	-	+	-	+	-	+	-	+

DIRECTIONS:

Assume that each of the above capital letters is the first letter of the name of a city using EAM equipment. The number directly beneath each capital letter is the code number for the city. The small letter beneath each code number is the code letter for the number of EAM divisions in the city and the + or - symbol directly beneath each code letter is the code symbol which signifies whether or not the city uses third generation computers with the EAM equipment.

The questions that follow show City Letters in Column I, Code Numbers in Column II, Code Letters in Column III, and Code Symbols in Column IV. If correct, each City Letter in Column I should correspond by position with each of the three codes shown in the other three columns, in accordance with the coding key shown above. *BUT* there are some errors. For each question,

If there is a total of *ONE* error in Columns 2, 3, and 4, mark your answer A.

If there is a total of *TWO* errors in Columns 2, 3, and 4, mark your answer B.

If there is a total of *THREE* errors in Columns 2, 3, and 4, mark your answer C.

If Columns 2, 3, and 4 are correct, mark your answer D.

SAMPLE QUESTION

I City Letter	II Code Numbers	III Code Letters	IV Code Symbols
Y J M O S	5 3 7 9 8	e b g i h	- - + + -

The errors are as follows: In Column 2, the Code Number should be "2" instead of "3" for City Letter "J," and in Column 4 the Code Symbol should be "+" instead of "-" for City Letter "Y." Since there is a total of two errors in Columns 2, 3, and 4, the answer to this sample question is B.

Now answer questions 1 through 9 according to these rules.

	I City Letters	II Code Numbers	III Code Letters	IV Code Symbols	
1.	K O R M P	6 9 3 7 1	f i e g a	- - + + +	1. ...
2.	O T P S Y	9 4 1 8 6	b d a h e	+ - - - +	2. ...
3.	R S J T M	3 8 1 4 7	c h b e g	- - - - +	3. ...
4.	P M S K J	1 7 8 6 2	a g h f b	+ + - - -	4. ...
5.	M Y T J R	7 5 4 2 3	g e d f c	+ + - - +	5. ...
6.	T P K Y O	4 1 6 7 9	d a f e i	- + - + -	6. ...
7.	S K O R T	8 6 9 3 5	h f i c d	- - + + -	7. ...
8.	J R Y P K	2 3 5 1 9	b d e a f	- + + + -	8. ...
9.	R O M P Y	4 9 7 1 5	c i g a d	+ + - + +	9. ...

TEST 6

CODE TABLE

Name of Offense	V A N D S B R U G H
Code Letter	c o m p l e x i t y
File Number	1 2 3 4 5 6 7 8 9 0

Assume that each of the above capital letters is the first letter of the name of an offense, that the small letter directly beneath each capital letter is the code letter for the offense, and that the number directly beneath each code letter is the file number for the offense.

DIRECTIONS: In each of the following questions, the code letters and file numbers should correspond to the capital letters.

If there is an error only in Column 2, mark your answer A.
If there is an error only in Column 3, mark your answer B.
If there is an error in both Column 2 and Column 3, mark your answer C.
If both Columns 2 and 3 are correct, mark your answer D.

SAMPLE QUESTION

Column 1	Column 2	Column 3
BNARGHSVVU	emoxtylcci	6357905118

The code letters in Column 2 are correct but the first "5" in Column 3 should be "2." Therefore, the answer is B. Now answer the following questions according to the above rules.

	Column 1	Column 2	Column 3	
1.	HGDSBNBSVR	ytplxmelcx	0945736517	1. ...
2.	SDGUUNHVAH	lptiimycoy	5498830120	2. ...
3.	BRSNAAVUDU	exlmooctpi	6753221848	3. ...
4.	VSRUDNADUS	cleipmopil	1568432485	4. ...
5.	NDSHVRBUAG	mplycxeiot	3450175829	5. ...
6.	GHUSNVBRDA	tyilmcexpo	9085316742	6. ...
7.	DBSHVURANG	pesycixomt	4650187239	7. ...
8.	RHNNASBDGU	xymnolepti	7033256398	8. ...

TEST 7

CODE TABLE

Code Letter	b	d	f	a	g	s	z	w	h	u
Code Number	1	2	3	4	5	6	7	8	9	0

In the Code Table above, each code letter has a corresponding code number directly beneath it.

DIRECTIONS: Each of the following questions contains three sets of code letters and code numbers. In each set, the code numbers should correspond with the code letters as given in the Table, but there is a coding error in some of the sets. Examine the sets in each question carefully.

Mark your answer A if there is a coding error in only *ONE* of the sets in the question.
Mark your answer B if there is a coding error in any *TWO* of the sets in the question.
Mark your answer C if there is a coding error in all *THREE* sets in the question.
Mark your answer D if there is a coding error in *NONE* of the sets in the question.

SAMPLE QUESTION

```
fgzduwaf - 35720843
uabsdgfw - 04262538
hhfaudgs - 99340257
```

In the above sample question, the first set is right because each code number matches the code letter as in the Code Table. In the second set, the corresponding number for the code letter b is wrong because it should be 1 instead of 2. In the third set, the corresponding number for the last code letter s is wrong because it should be 6 instead of 7. Since there is an error in two of the sets, the answer to the above sample question is B.

1.	fsbughwz - 36104987	zwubgasz - 78025467	1. ...
	ghgufddb - 59583221		
2.	hafgdaas - 94351446	ddsfabsd - 22734162	2. ...
	wgdbssgf - 85216553		
3.	abfbssbd - 41316712	ghzfaubs - 59734017	3. ...
	sdbzfwza - 62173874		
4.	whfbdzag - 89412745	daaszuub - 24467001	4. ...
	uzhfwssd - 07936623		
5.	zbadgbuh - 71425109	dzadbbsz - 27421167	5. ...
	gazhwaff - 54798433		
6.	fbfuadsh - 31304265	gzfuwzsb - 57300671	
	bashhgag - 14699535		

TEST 8

DIRECTIONS: The following questions are to be answered on the basis of the following Code Table. In this table every letter has a corresponding code number to be punched. Each question contains three pairs of letters and code numbers. In each pair, the code numbers should correspond with the letters in accordance with the Code Table.

CODE TABLE

Letter	P	L	A	N	D	C	O	B	U	R
Corresponding Code Number	1	2	3	4	5	6	7	8	9	0

In some of the pairs below, an error exists in the coding. Examine the pairs in each question. Mark your answer

    A if there is a mistake in only *one* of the pairs
    B if there is a mistake in only *two* of the pairs
    C if there is a mistake in *all three* of the pairs
    D if there is a mistake in *none* of the pairs

SAMPLE QUESTION

        LCBPUPAB - 26819138
        ACOABOL - 3683872
        NDURONUC - 46901496

In the above sample, the first pair is correct since each letter as listed has the correct corresponding code number. In the second pair, an error exists because the letter O should have the code number 7, instead of 8. In the third pair, an error exists because the letter D should have the code number 5, instead of 6. Since there are errors in two of the three pairs, your answer should be B.

1.	ADCANPLC - 35635126	DORURBBO - 57090877	1. ...
	PNACBUCP - 14368061		
2.	LCOBLRAP - 26782931	UPANUPCD - 91349156	2. ...
	RLDACLRO - 02536207		
3.	LCOROPAR - 26707130	BALANRUP - 83234091	3. ...
	DOPOAULL - 57173922		
4.	ONCRUBAP - 74609831	DCLANORD - 56243705	4. ...
	AORPDUR - 3771590		
5.	PANRBUCD - 13408965	UAOCDPLR - 93765120	5. ...
	OPDDOBRA - 71556803		
6.	BAROLDCP - 83072561	PNOCOBLA - 14767823	6. ...
	BURPDOLA - 89015723		
7.	ANNCPABO - 34461387	DBALDRCP - 58325061	7. ...
	ACRPOUL - 3601792		
8.	BLAPOUR - 8321790	NOACNPL - 4736412	8. ...
	RODACORD - 07536805		

8

9. ADUBURCL - 3598062   NOCOBAPR - 47578310   9. ...
    PRONDALU - 10754329
10. UBADCLOR - 98356270   NBUPPARA - 48911033   10. ...
    LONDUPRC - 27459106

TEST 9

DIRECTIONS: Answer questions 1 through 10 ONLY on the basis of the following information.

Column I consists of serial numbers of dollar bills. Column II shows different ways of arranging the corresponding serial numbers.

The serial numbers of dollar bills in Column I begin and end with a capital letter and have an eight-digit number in between. The serial numbers in Column I are to be arranged according to the following rules:

FIRST: In alphabetical order according to the first letter.

SECOND: When two or more serial numbers have the same first letter, in alphabetical order according to the last letter.

THIRD: When two or more serial numbers have the same first and last letters, in numerical order, beginning with the lowest number.

The serial numbers in Column I are numbered (1) through (5) in the order in which they are listed. In Column II the numbers (1) through (5) are arranged in four different ways to show different arrangements of the corresponding serial numbers. Choose the answer in Column II in which the serial numbers are arranged according to the above rules.

SAMPLE QUESTION

COLUMN I	COLUMN II
(1) E75044127B	(A) 4,1,3,2,5
(2) B96399104A	(B) 4,1,2,3,5
(3) B93939086A	(C) 4,3,2,5,1
(4) B47064465H	(D) 3,2,5,4,1
(5) B99040922A	

In the sample question, the four serial numbers starting with B should be put before the serial number starting with E. The serial numbers starting with B and ending with A should be put before the serial number starting with B and ending with H. The three serial numbers starting with B and ending with A should be listed in numerical order, beginning with the lowest number. The correct way to arrange the serial numbers, therefore, is:

        (3) B93939086A
        (2) B96399104A
        (5) B99040922A
        (4) B47064465H
        (1) E75044127B

Since the order of arrangement is 3, 2, 5, 4, 1, the answer to the sample question is (D).

	COLUMN I		COLUMN II
1.	(1) P44343314Y	A.	2,3,1,4,5
	(2) P44141341S	B.	1,5,3,2,4
	(3) P44141431L	C.	4,2,3,5,1
	(4) P41143413W	D.	5,3,2,4,1
	(5) P44313433H		
2.	(1) D89077275M	A.	3,2,5,4,1
	(2) D98073724N	B.	1,4,3,2,5
	(3) D90877274N	C.	4,1,5,2,3
	(4) D98877275M	D.	1,3,2,5,4
	(5) D98873725N		

9

	COLUMN I		COLUMN II
3.	(1) H32548137E	A.	2,4,5,1,3
	(2) H35243178A	B.	1,5,2,3,4
	(3) H35284378F	C.	1,5,2,4,3
	(4) H35288337A	D.	2,1,5,3,4
	(5) H32883173B		
4.	(1) K24165039H	A.	4,2,5,3,1
	(2) F24106599A	B.	2,3,4,1,5
	(3) L21406639G	C.	4,2,5,1,3
	(4) C24156093A	D.	1,3,4,5,2
	(5) K24165593D		
5.	(1) H79110642E	A.	2,1,3,5,4
	(2) H79101928E	B.	2,1,4,5,3
	(3) A79111567F	C.	3,5,2,1,4
	(4) H79111796E	D.	4,3,5,1,2
	(5) A79111618F		
6.	(1) P16388385W	A.	3,4,5,2,1
	(2) R16388335V	B.	2,3,4,5,1
	(3) P16383835W	C.	2,4,3,1,5
	(4) R18386865V	D.	3,1,5,2,4
	(5) P18686865W		
7.	(1) B42271749G	A.	4,1,5,2,3
	(2) B42271779G	B.	4,1,2,5,3
	(3) E43217779G	C.	1,2,4,5,3
	(4) B42874119C	D.	5,3,1,2,4
	(5) E42817749G		
8.	(1) M57906455S	A.	4,1,5,3,2
	(2) N87077758S	B.	3,4,1,5,2
	(3) N87707757B	C.	4,1,5,2,3
	(4) M57877759B	D.	1,5,3,2,4
	(5) M57906555S		
9.	(1) C69336894Y	A.	2,5,3,1,4
	(2) C69336684V	B.	3,2,5,1,4
	(3) C69366887W	C.	3,1,4,5,2
	(4) C69366994Y	D.	2,5,1,3,4
	(5) C69336865V		
10.	(1) A56247181D	A.	1,5,3,2,4
	(2) A56272128P	B.	3,1,5,2,4
	(3) H56247128D	C.	3,2,1,5,4
	(4) H56272288P	D.	1,5,2,3,4
	(5) A56247188D		

———

TEST 10

DIRECTIONS: Answer the following questions on the basis of the instructions, the code, and the sample questions given below. Assume that an officer at a certain location is equipped with a two-way radio to keep him in constant touch with his security headquarters. Radio messages and replies are given in code form, as follows:

CODE TABLE

Radio Code for Situation	J	P	M	F	B
Radio Code for Action to be Taken	o	r	a	z	q
Radio Response for Action Being Taken	1	2	3	4	5

Assume that each of the above capital letters is the radio code for a particular type of situation, that the small letter below each capital letter is the radio code for the action an officer is directed to take, and that the number directly below each small letter is the radio response an officer should make to indicate what action was actually taken.

In each of the following questions, the code letter for the action directed (Column 2) and the code number for the action taken (Column 3) should correspond to the capital letters in Column 1.

INSTRUCTIONS: If only Column 2 is different from Column 1, mark your answer I.
If only Column 3 is different from Column 1, mark your answer II.
If both Column 2 and Column 3 are different from Column I, mark your answer III.
If both Columns 2 and 3 are the same as Column 1, mark your answer IV.

SAMPLE QUESTION

Column 1	Column 2	Column 3
JPFMB	orzaq	12453

The CORRECT answer is: A. I   B. II   C. III   D. IV

The code letters in Column 2 are correct, but the numbers "53" in Column 3 should be "35." Therefore, the answer is B. Now answer the following questions according to the above rules.

	Column 1	Column 2	Column 3	
1.	PBFJM	rqzoa	25413	1. ___
2.	MPFBJ	zrqao	32541	2. ___
3.	JBFPM	oqzra	15432	3. ___
4.	BJPMF	qaroz	51234	4. ___
5.	PJFMB	rozaq	21435	5. ___
6.	FJBMP	zoqra	41532	6. ___

KEYS (CORRECT ANSWERS)

TEST 1		TEST 2		TEST 3		TEST 4		TEST 5	
1.	B	1.	B	1.	D	1.	A	1.	B
2.	C	2.	D	2.	C	2.	C	2.	C
3.	D	3.	C	3.	A	3.	B	3.	C
4.	A	4.	D	4.	B	4.	B	4.	D
5.	C	5.	A	5.	A	5.	D	5.	A
		6.	C	6.	D	6.	C	6.	B
		7.	D	7.	B	7.	B	7.	A
		8.	B	8.	C			8.	B
								9.	C

TEST 6		TEST 7		TEST 8		TEST 9		TEST 10	
1.	C	1.	B	1.	C	1.	D	1.	D
2.	D	2.	C	2.	B	2.	B	2.	C
3.	A	3.	B	3.	D	3.	A	3.	B
4.	C	4.	B	4.	B	4.	C	4.	A
5.	B	5.	D	5.	A	5.	C	5.	D
6.	D	6.	C	6.	D	6.	D	6.	A
7.	A			7.	B	7.	B		
8.	C			8.	B	8.	A		
				9.	C	9.	A		
				10.	A	10.	D		

PREPARING WRITTEN MATERIAL
EXAMINATION SECTION

DIRECTIONS FOR TESTS 1-8:
  Each of the sentences in the Tests that follow may be classified under one of the following four categories:
  A. *Faulty* because of incorrect grammar or word usage
  B. *Faulty* because of incorrect punctuation
  C. *Faulty* because of incorrect capitalization or incorrect spelling
  D. *Correct*
Examine each sentence carefully to determine under which of the above four options it is best classified. Then, in the space to the right, print the capital letter preceding the option which is the best of the four suggested above.
  (Note that each faulty sentence contains but one type of error. Consider a sentence to be correct if it contains none of the types of errors mentioned, even though there may be other correct ways of expressing the same thought.)

___

TEST 1

1. He sent the notice to the clerk who you hired yesterday.   1. ...
2. It must be admitted, however that you were not informed   2. ...
   of this change.
3. Only the employees who have served in this grade for at   3. ...
   least two years are eligible for promotion.
4. The work was divided equally between she and Mary.   4. ...
5. He thought that you were not available at that time.   5. ...
6. When the messenger returns; please give him this package.   6. ...
7. The new secretary prepared, typed, addressed, and de-   7. ...
   livered, the notices.
8. Walking into the room, his desk can be seen at the rear.   8. ...
9. Although John has worked here longer than She, he produces   9. ...
   a smaller amount of work.
10. She said she could of typed this report yesterday.   10. ...
11. Neither one of these procedures are adequate for the ef-   11. ...
    ficient performance of this task.
12. The typewriter is the tool of the typist; the cashe   12. ...
    register, the tool of the cashier.
13. "The assignment must be completed as soon as possible"   13. ...
    said the supervisor.
14. As you know, office handbooks are issued to all new Em-   14. ...
    ployees.
15. Writing a speech is sometimes easier than to deliver it   15. ...
    before an audience.
16. Mr. Brown our accountant, will audit the accounts next   16. ...
    week.
17. Give the assignment to whomever is able to do it most   17. ...
    efficiently.
18. The supervisor expected either your or I to file these   18. ...
    reports.

___

TEST 2

1. The fire apparently started in the storeroom, which is   1. ...
   usually locked.

1

2. On approaching the victim two bruises were noticed by   2. ...
this officer.
3. The officer, who was there examined the report with great   3. ...
care.
4. Each employee in the office had a seperate desk.   4. ...
5. All employees including members of the clerical staff,   5. ...
were invited to the lecture.
6. The suggested Procedure is similar to the one now in use.   6. ...
7. No one was more pleased with the new procedure than the   7. ...
chauffeur.
8. He tried to persaude her to change the procedure.   8. ...
9. The total of the expenses charged to petty cash were high.   9. ...
10. An understanding between him and I was finally reached.   10. ...

TEST 3

1. They told both he and I that the prisoner had escaped.   1. ...
2. Any superior officer, who, disregards the just complaints   2. ...
of his subordinates, is remiss in the performance of his
duty.
3. Only those members of the national organization who resided   3. ...
in the Middle West attended the conference in Chicago.
4. We told him to give the investigation assignment to who-   4. ...
ever was available.
5. Please do not disappoint and embarass us by not appearing   5. ...
in court.
6. Although the officer's speech proved to be entertaining,   6. ...
the topic was not relevent to the main theme of the conference.
7. In February all new officers attended a training course   7. ...
in which they were learned in their principal duties and
the fundamental operating procedures of the department.
8. I personally seen inmate Jones threaten inmates Smith and   8. ...
Green with bodily harm if they refused to participate in
the plot.
9. To the layman, who on a chance visit to the prison ob-   9. ...
serves everything functioning smoothly, the maintenance
of prison discipline may seem to be a relatively easily
realizable objective.
10. The prisoners in cell block fourty were forbidden to sit   10. ...
on the cell cots during the recreation hour.

TEST 4

1. I cannot encourage you any.   1. ...
2. You always look well in those sort of clothes.   2. ...
3. Shall we go to the park?   3. ...
4. The man whome he introduced was Mr. Carey.   4. ...
5. She saw the letter laying here this morning.   5. ...
6. It should rain before the Afternoon is over.   6. ...
7. They have already went home.   7. ...
8. That Jackson will be elected is evident.   8. ...
9. He does not hardly approve of us.   9. ...
10. It was he, who won the prize.   10. ...

TEST 5

1.	Shall we go to the park.	1.	...
2.	They are, alike, in this particular.	2.	...
3.	They gave the poor man sume food when he knocked on the door.	3.	...
4.	I regret the loss caused by the error.	4.	...
5.	The students' will have a new teacher.	5.	...
6.	They sweared to bring out all the facts.	6.	...
7.	He decided to open a branch store on 33rd street.	7.	...
8.	His speed is equal and more than that of a racehorse.	8.	...
9.	He felt very warm on that Summer day.	9.	...
10.	He was assisted by his friend, who lives in the next house.	10.	...

TEST 6

1.	The climate of New York is colder than California.	1.	...
2.	I shall wait for you on the corner.	2.	...
3.	Did we see the boy who, we think, is the leader.	3.	...
4.	Being a modest person, John seldom talks about his invention.	4.	...
5.	The gang is called the smith street boys.	5.	...
6.	He seen the man break into the store.	6.	...
7.	We expected to lay still there for quite a while.	7.	...
8.	He is considered to be the Leader of his organization.	8.	...
9.	Although I recieved an invitation, I won't go.	9.	...
10.	The letter must be here some place.	10.	...

TEST 7

1.	I though it to be he.	1.	...
2.	We expect to remain here for a long time.	2.	...
3.	The committee was agreed.	3.	...
4.	Two-thirds of the building are finished.	4.	...
5.	The water was froze.	5.	...
6.	Everyone of the salesmen must supply their own car.	6.	...
7.	Who is the author of Gone With the Wind?	7.	...
8.	He marched on and declaring that he would never surrender.	8.	...
9.	Who shall I say called?	9.	...
10.	Everyone has left but they.	10.	...

TEST 8

1.	Who did we give the order to?	1.	...
2.	Send your order in immediately.	2.	...
3.	I believe I paid the Bill.	3.	...
4.	I have not met but one person.	4.	...
5.	Why aren't Tom, and Fred, going to the dance?	5.	...
6.	What reason is there for him not going?	6.	...
7.	The seige of Malta was a tremendous event.	7.	...
8.	I was there yesterday I assure you.	8.	...
9.	Your ukelele is better than mine.	9.	...
10.	No one was there only Mary.	10.	...

TEST 9

DIRECTIONS FOR TEST 9:

In each of the following groups of sentences, one of the four sentences is faulty in grammar, punctuation, or capitalization. Select the incorrect sentence in each case.

1. A. If you had stood at home and done your homework, you   1. ...
      would not have failed in arithmetic.
   B. Her affected manner annoyed every member of the audience.
   C. How will the new law affect our income taxes?
   D. The plants were not affected by the long, cold winter,
      but they succumbed to the drought of summer.
2. A. He is one of the most able men who have been in the   2. ...
      Senate.
   B. It is he who is to blame for the lamentable mistake.
   C. Haven't you a helpful suggestion to make at this time?
   D. The money was robbed from the blind man's cup.
3. A. The amount of children in this school is steadily in-   3. ...
      creasing.
   B. After taking an apple from the table, she went out to play.
   C. He borrowed a dollar from me.
   D. I had hoped my brother would arrive before me.
4. A. Whom do you think I hear from every week?   4. ...
   B. Who do you think is the right man for the job?
   C. Who do you think I found in the room?
   D. He is the man whom we considered a good candidate for
      the presidency.
5. A. Quietly the puppy laid down before the fireplace.   5. ...
   B. You have made your bed; now lie in it.
   C. I was badly sunburned because I had lain too long in the
      sun.
   D. I laid the doll on the bed and left the room.

KEYS (CORRECT ANSWERS)

TEST 1		TEST 2	TEST 3	TEST 4	TEST 5
1. A	10. A	1. D	1. A	1. A	1. B
2. B	11. A	2. A	2. B	2. A	2. B
3. D	12. C	3. B	3. C	3. D	3. C
4. A	13. B	4. C	4. D	4. C	4. D
5. D	14. C	5. B	5. C	5. A	5. B
6. B	15. A	6. C	6. C	6. C	6. A
7. B	16. B	7. D	7. A	7. A	7. C
8. A	17. A	8. C	8. A	8. D	8. A
9. C	18. A	9. A	9. D	9. A	9. C
		10. A	10. C	10. B	10. D

TEST 6	TEST 7	TEST 8	TEST 9
1. A	1. A	1. A	1. A
2. D	2. D	2. D	2. D
3. B	3. D	3. C	3. A
4. D	4. A	4. A	4. C
5. C	5. A	5. B	5. A
6. A	6. A	6. A	
7. A	7. B	7. C	
8. C	8. A	8. B	
9. C	9. D	9. C	
10. A	10. D	10. A	

PREPARING WRITTEN MATERIAL

PARAGRAPH REARRANGEMENT

COMMENTARY

The sentences which follow are in scrambled order. You are to rearrange them in proper order and indicate the letter choice containing the correct answer at the space at the right.

Each group of sentences in this section is actually a paragraph presented in scrambled order. Each sentence in the group has a place in that paragraph; no sentence is to be left out. You are to read each group of sentences and decide upon the best order in which to put the sentences so as to form as well-organized paragraph.

The questions in this section measure the ability to solve a problem when all the facts relevant to its solution are not given.

More specifically, certain positions of responsibility and authority require the employee to discover connections between events sometimes, apparently, unrelated. In order to do this, the employee will find it necessary to correctly infer that unspecified events have probably occurred or are likely to occur. This ability becomes especially important when action must be taken on incomplete information.

Accordingly, these questions require competitors to choose among several suggested alternatives, each of which presents a different sequential arrangement of the events. Competitors must choose the MOST logical of the suggested sequences.

In order to do so, they may be required to draw on general knowledge to infer missing concepts or events that are essential to sequencing the given events. Competitors should be careful to infer only what is essential to the sequence. The plausibility of the wrong alternatives will always require the inclusion of unlikely events or of additional chains of events which are NOT essential to sequencing the given events.

It's very important to remember that you are looking for the best of the four possible choices, and that the best choice of all may not even be one of the answers you're given to choose from.

There is no one right way to these problems. Many people have found it helpful to first write out the order of the sentences, as they would have arranged them, on their scrap paper before looking at the possible answers. If their optimum answer is there, this can save them some time. If it isn't, this method can still give insight into solving the problem. Others find it most helpful to just go through each of the possible choices, contrasting each as they go along. You should use whatever method feels comfortable, and works, for you.

While most of these types of questions are not that difficult, we've added a higher percentage of the difficult type, just to give you more practice. Usually there are only one or two questions on this section that contain such subtle distinctions that you're unable to answer confidently, and you then may find yourself stuck deciding between two possible choices, neither of which you're sure about.

EXAMINATION SECTION

TEST 1

DIRECTIONS: The sentences that follow are in scrambled order. You are to rearrange them in proper order and indicate the letter choice containing the correct answer. *PRINT THE LETTER OF THE CORRECT ANSWER IN THE SPACE AT THE RIGHT.*

1. Below are four statements labeled W.,X.,Y.,and Z.   1. ___
   W. He was a strict and fanatic drillmaster.
   X. The word is always used in a derogatory sense and generally shows resentment and anger on the part of the user.
   Y. It is from the name of this Frenchman that we derive our English word, martinet.
   Z. Jean Martinet was the Inspector-General of Infantry during the reign of King Louis XIV.

   The *PROPER* order in which these sentences should be placed in a paragraph is:
   A. X,Z,W,Y   B. X,Z,Y,W   C. Z,W,Y,X   D. Z,Y,W,X

2. In the following paragraph, the sentences which are num-   2. ___
   bered, have been jumbled.
   (1) Since then it has undergone changes.
   (2) It was incorporated in 1955 under the laws of the State of New York.
   (3) Its primary purpose, a cleaner city, has, however, remained the same.
   (4) The Citizens Committee works in cooperation with the Mayor's Inter-departmental Committee for a Clean City.

   The order in which these sentences should be arranged to form a well-organized paragraph is:
   A. 2,4,1,3   B. 3,4,1,2   C. 4,2,1,3   D. 4,3,2,1

Questions 3-5.

DIRECTIONS: The sentences listed below are part of a meaningful paragraph but they are not given in their proper order. You are to decide what would be the *best order* in which to put the sentences so as to form a well-organized paragraph. Each sentence has a place in the paragraph; there are no extra sentences. You are then to answer questions 3 to 5 inclusive on the basis of your rearrangements of these secrambled sentences into a properly organized paragraph.

In 1887 some insurance companies organized an Inspection Department to advise their clients on all phases of fire prevention and protection. Probably this has been due to the smaller annual fire losses in Great Britain than in the United States. It tests various fire prevention devices and appliances and determines manufacturing hazards and their safeguards. Fire research began earlier in the United States and is more advanced than in Great Britain. Later they established a laboratory specializing in electrical, mechanical, hydraulic, and chemical fields.

3. When the five sentences are arranged in proper order, the   3. ___
   paragraph starts with the sentence which begins
   A. "In 1887 ...." B. "Probably this ..." C. "It tests ..."
   D. "Fire research ..."   E. "Later they ..."

4. In the last sentence listed above, "they" refers to   4. ___
   A. insurance companies   B. the United States
   B. the United States and Great Britain
   C. the Inspection Department
   D. clients
   E. technicians

5. When the above paragraph is properly arranged, it ends with   5. ___
   the words
   A. "... and protection."   B. "... the United States."
   C. "... their safeguards."   D. "... in Great Britain."
   E. "... chemical fields."

———

KEY (CORRECT ANSWERS)

1.   C
2.   C
3.   D
4.   A
5.   C

———

TEST 2

DIRECTIONS: In each of the questions numbered 1 through 5, several sentences are given. For each question, choose as your answer the group of numbers that represents the *most logical* order of these sentences if they were arranged in paragraph form. *PRINT THE LETTER OF THE CORRECT ANSWER IN THE SPACE AT THE RIGHT.*

1.
1. It is established when one shows that the landlord has prevented the tenant's enjoyment of his interest in the property leased.
2. Constructive eviction is the result of a breach of the covenant of quiet enjoyment implied in all leases.
3. In some parts of the United States, it is not complete until the tenant vacates within a reasonable time.
4. Generally, the acts must be of such serious and permanent character as to deny the tenant the enjoyment of his possessing rights.
5. In this event, upon abandonment of the premises, the tenant's liability for that ceases.

1. ___

The CORRECT answer is:
   A. 2,1,4,3,5   B. 5,2,3,1,4   C. 4,3,1,2,5
   D. 1,3,5,4,2

2.
1. The powerlessness before private and public authorities that is the typical experience of the slum tenant is reminiscent of the situation of blue-collar workers all through the nineteenth century.
2. Similarly, in recent years, this chapter of history has been reopened by anti-poverty groups which have attempted to organize slum tenants to enable them to bargain collectively with their landlords about the conditions of their tenancies.
3. It is familiar history that many of the workers remedied their condition by joining together and presenting their demands collectively.
4. Like the workers, tenants are forced by the conditions of modern life into substantial dependence on these who possess great political and economic power.
5. What's more, the very fact of dependence coupled with an absence of education and self-confidence makes them hesitant and unable to stand up for what they need from those in power.

2. ___

The CORRECT answer is:
   A. 5,4,1,2,3   B. 2,3,1,5,4   C. 3,1,5,4,2
   D. 1,4,5,3,2

2 (#2)

3 1. A railroad, for example, when not acting as a common
       carrier may contract away responsibility for its own
       negligence.
    2. As to a landlord, however, no decision has been found
       relating to the legal effect of a clause shifting the
       statutory duty of repair to the tenant.
    3. The courts have not passed on the validity of clauses
       relieving the landlord of this duty and liability.
    4. They have, however, upheld the validity of exculpatory
       clauses in other types of contracts.
    5. Housing regulations impose a duty upon the landlord to
       maintain leased premises in safe condition.
    6. As another example, a bailee may limit his liability ex-
       cept for gross negligence, willful acts, or fraud.

   The CORRECT answer is:
     A. 2,1,6,4,3,5   B. 1,3,4,5,6,2   C. 3,5,1,4,2,6
     D. 5,3,4,1,6,2

3. ___

4. 1. Since there are only samples in the building, retail
       or consumer sales are generally eschewed by mart occu-
       pants, and, in some instances, rigid controls are main-
       tained to limit entrance to the mart only to those per-
       sons engaged in retailing.
    2. Since World War I, in many larger cities, there has de-
       veloped a new type of property, called the mart building.
    3. It can therefore be used by wholesalers and jobbers for
       the display of sample merchandise.
    4. This type of building is most frequently a multi-storied,
       finished interior property which is a cross between a re-
       tail arcade and a loft building.
    5. This limitation enables the mart occupants to ship the
       orders from another location after the retailer or dealer
       makes his selection from the samples.

   The CORRECT answer is:
     A. 2,4,3,1,5   B. 4,3,5,1,2   C. 1,3,2,4,5
     D. 1,4,2,3,5

4. ___

5. 1. In general, staff-line friction reduces the distinctive
       contribution of staff personnel.
    2. The conflicts, however, introduce an uncontrolled element
       into the managerial system.
    3. On the other hand, the natural resistance of the line to
       staff innovations probably usefully restrains over-eager
       efforts to apply untested procedures on a large scale.
    4. Under such conditions, it is difficult to know when valu-
       able ideas are being sacrificed.
    5. The relatively weak position of staff, requiring accommo-
       dation to the line, tends to restrict their ability to
       engage in free, experimental innovation.

   The CORRECT answer is:
     A. 4,2,3,1,3   B. 1,5,3,2,4   C. 5,3,1,2,4
     D. 2,1,4,5,3

5. ___

KEY (CORRECT ANSWERS)

1. A
2. D
3. D
4. A
5. B

———

TEST 3

DIRECTIONS: Questions 1 through 4 consist of six sentences which can be arranged in a logical sequence. For each question, select the choice which places the numbered sentences in the *most logical* sequence. *PRINT THE LETTER OF THE CORRECT ANSWER IN THE SPACE AT THE RIGHT.*

1. 1. The burden of proof as to each issue is determined before trial and remains upon the same party throughout the trial.
   2. The jury is at liberty to believe one witness' testimony as against a number of contradictory witnesses.
   3. In a civil case, the party bearing the burden of proof is required to prove his contention by a fair preponderance of the evidence.
   4. However, it must be noted that a fair preponderance of evidence does not necessarily mean a greater number of witnesses.
   5. The burden of proof is the burden which rests upon one of the parties to an action to persuade the trier of the facts, generally the jury, that a proposition he asserts is true.
   6. If the evidence is equally balanced, or if it leaves the jury in such doubt as to be unable to decide the controversy either way, judgment must be given against the party upon whom the burden of proof rests.

   The CORRECT answer is:
   A. 3,2,5,4,1,6   B. 1,2,6,5,3,4   C. 3,4,5,1,2,6
   D. 5,1,3,6,4,2

   1. ___

2. 1. If a parent is without assets and is unemployed, he cannot be convicted of the crime of non-support of a child.
   2. The term "sufficient ability" has been held to mean sufficient financial ability.
   3. It does not matter if his unemployment is by choice or unavoidable circumstances.
   4. If he fails to take any steps at all, he may be liable to prosecution for endangering the welfare of a child.
   5. Under the penal law, a parent is responsible for the support of his minor child only if the parent is "of sufficient ability,"
   6. An indigent parent may meet his obligation by borrowing money or by seeking aid under the provisions of the Social Welfare Law.

   The CORRECT answer is:
   A. 6,1,5,3,2,4   B. 1,3,5,2,4,6   C. 5,2,1,3,6,4
   D. 1,6,4,5,2,3

   2. ___

3. 1. Consider, for example, the case of a rabble rouser   3. ___
      who urges a group of twenty people to go out and break
      the windows of a nearby factory.
   2. Therefore, the law fills the indicated gap with the crime
      of "inciting to riot."   .
   3. A person is considered guilty of inciting to riot when he
      urges ten or more persons to engage · in tumultuous and vio-
      lent conduct of a kind likely to create public alarm.
   4. However, if he has not obtained the cooperation of at least
      four people, he cannot be charged with unlawful assembly.
   5. The charge of inciting to riot was added to the law to cover
      types of conduct which cannot be classified as either the
      crime of "riot" or the crime of "unlawful assembly."
   6. If he acquires the acquiescence of at least four of them,
      he is guilty of unlawful assembly even if the project does
      not materialize.

   The CORRECT answer is:
     A. 3,5,1,6,4,2   B. 5,1,4,6,2,3   C. 3,4,1,5,2,6
     D. 5,1,4,6,3,2

4. 1. If, however, the rebuttal evidence presents an issue of   4. ___
      credibility, it is for the jury to determine whether the
      presumption has, in fact, been destroyed.
   2. Once sufficient evidence to the contrary is introduced,
      the presumption disappears from the trial.
   3. The effect of a presumption is to place the burden upon
      the adversary to come forward with evidence to rebut the
      presumption.
   4. When a presumption is overcome and ceases to exist in the
      case, the fact or facts which gave rise to the presumption
      still remain.
   5. Whether a presumption has been overcome is ordinarily a
      question for the court.
   6. Such information may furnish a basis for a logical inference.

   The CORRECT answer is:
     A. 4,6,2,5,1,3   B. 3,2,5,1,4,6   C. 5,3,6,4,2,1
     D. 5,4,1,2,6,3

   ———

KEY (CORRECT ANSWERS)

     1.   D
     2.   C
     3.   A
     4.   B

   ———

ANSWER SHEET

USE THE SPECIAL PENCIL.   MAKE GLOSSY BLACK MARKS.

	A B C D E		A B C D E		A B C D E		A B C D E		A B C D E
1		26		51		76		101	
2		27		52		77		102	
3		28		53		78		103	
4		29		54		79		104	
5		30		55		80		105	
6		31		56		81		106	
7		32		57		82		107	
8		33		58		83		108	
9		34		59		84		109	
10		35		60		85		110	

Make only ONE mark for each answer.   Additional and stray marks may be
counted as mistakes.   In making corrections, erase errors COMPLETELY.

	A B C D E		A B C D E		A B C D E		A B C D E		A B C D E
11		36		61		86		111	
12		37		62		87		112	
13		38		63		88		113	
14		39		64		89		114	
15		40		65		90		115	
16		41		66		91		116	
17		42		67		92		117	
18		43		68		93		118	
19		44		69		94		119	
20		45		70		95		120	
21		46		71		96		121	
22		47		72		97		122	
23		48		73		98		123	
24		49		74		99		124	
25		50		75		100		125	

ANSWER SHEET

TEST NO. _____ PART _____ TITLE OF POSITION _____

PLACE OF EXAMINATION _____ DATE_____

(CITY OR TOWN)   (STATE)

RATING

USE THE SPECIAL PENCIL.   MAKE GLOSSY BLACK MARKS.

	A B C D E		A B C D E		A B C D E		A B C D E		A B C D E
1		26		51		76		101	
2		27		52		77		102	
3		28		53		78		103	
4		29		54		79		104	
5		30		55		80		105	
6		31		56		81		106	
7		32		57		82		107	
8		33		58		83		108	
9		34		59		84		109	
10		35		60		85		110	

Make only ONE mark for each answer. Additional and stray marks may be counted as mistakes. In making corrections, erase errors COMPLETELY.

	A B C D E		A B C D E		A B C D E		A B C D E		A B C D E
11		36		61		86		111	
12		37		62		87		112	
13		38		63		88		113	
14		39		64		89		114	
15		40		65		90		115	
16		41		66		91		116	
17		42		67		92		117	
18		43		68		93		118	
19		44		69		94		119	
20		45		70		95		120	
21		46		71		96		121	
22		47		72		97		122	
23		48		73		98		123	
24		49		74		99		124	
25		50		75		100		125	